WANT MORE

When you're ready, here are three other ways I can help you help yourself:

ONE: Learn from my KYN Learning Academy

Learn from our short video series why 'Knowing Your Numbers' will help you stop financial firefighting, cut your stress, and help grow your business.

knowyournumbers.biz/kyn-training-academy

TWO: Take the online Cash Flow Diagnostic Scorecard:

Are you ready to uncover the hidden risks in your cash flow? Answer 10 questions to find out.

kyncashflowdiagnostic.com

THREE: Take your learning to the next level and join a Know Your Numbers Mastery Group

Join Craig and a small group of other entrepreneurs on a journey to get less stress, more profit and to make better decisions.

knowyournumbers.biz/know-your-numbers-mastery-group

See you on the other side, Craig!

Lessons From the Rocking Chair

How Business Owners Can Master Their Entrepreneurial Journey Using Timeless Wisdom and Insight

Craig Alexander Rattray

Copyright © 2024 Craig Alexander Rattray Limited

All rights reserved. Without limiting the rights under copyright reserved above, no part of this book may be reproduced, stored, or introduced into a retrieval system, or transmitted, in any form or by any means (electronic, mechanical, photocopying, recording or otherwise), without the prior written permission of both the copyright owner and the publisher.

Published by Craig Alexander Rattray Limited

DISCLAIMER:

This book contains the opinions and ideas of the author. The purpose of this book is to provide you with helpful information. This book should not be relied upon solely to make decisions in your business. Careful attention has been paid to ensure the accuracy of the information, but the author cannot assume responsibility for the validity or consequences of its use. This information is not intended to be all things to all businesses. It is, by nature, generic to most businesses in general.

The material in this book is for informational purposes only. As each individual situation is unique, the author disclaims responsibility for any adverse effects that may result from the use or application of the information contained in this book. Any use of the information found in this book is the sole responsibility of the reader. Any suggestions found in this book are to be followed only after consultation with your own trusted advisors.

Dedicated to those brave men and women who have made the leap from employment to entrepreneurship. Remember, you are not alone!

If it was easy, everyone would be doing it and there would be no employees.

CONTENTS

PART 1: ROCKING CHAIR INTRODUCTION 2
    Welcome! 7
PART 2: ECONOMICS OF BUSINESS 10
    Understanding the Working Capital Cycle 12
    Delivering Value 13
    EBITDA 16
    Working Capital 18
    Growth 21
    Measuring Performance 22
    Where You Are, Where You Have Been, and Where You Are Going 23
    Differentiation 24
PART 3: NETWORKING AND RELATIONSHIPS 28
    Opportunities 30
    Keeping Funders Close 31
    Relationships 33
    Support 34
PART 4: TENACITY 36
    Time 38
    Time (after Time) 39
    Discipline 40
    Hard Work 43

It is Not Easy 44
PART 5: RESILIENCE 48
   Breakthroughs 50
   Pain 52
   Cash Flow Pain 54
   Struggling 55
   Change and Challenges 57
   Uncertainty 59
   Digging Deep 60
PART 6: EDUCATION 62
   Blossoming and Blooming 64
   Dreams 65
   Reflections 66
   Remembering 68
   Ambition 69
   Continuous Improvement 71
   Learning Greek 72
   Attitude & Outlook 74
   Action 75
   Why? 77
   Uncomfortable 78
PART 7: PROFITABILITY AND FINANCE 82
   Paying Yourself More 84
   Funding 86
   Health and Wealth 88

- PART 8: REJUVENATION 90
  - Freedom 92
  - Sleeping Soundly 94
  - Health 95
  - Feeling Tired 96
- PART 9: ETHICS 98
  - Do the Right Thing 100
- PART 10: NAVIGATION 102
  - Visibility 104
  - Juggling 105
  - Change 107
  - Evolving 108
  - Darkness 109
- PART 11: EMPOWERMENT 112
  - Gratitude 114
  - More Gratitude 114
  - Even More Gratitude 116
  - Dreams into Reality 117
  - Happiness 119
  - Listening 120
  - Fulfilment 121
  - You Get What You Tolerate 122
- PART 12: UNDERSTANDING 124
  - Measuring, Monitoring, and Managing 126
  - Feelings 127

    Responsibility 129

    Growing 131

    It Is Never Too Late 132

    Same Place Next Year 133

    Get It Done 134

    Focus on Yourself 136

    Success 137

    Control 138

PART 13: RESOURCEFULNESS 140

    Loneliness 142

    Opportunity 143

    I Am Back and I Am Giving Back 144

    Commitment 145

    All or Nothing 147

    Reflecting 149

    Lead a Horse to Water 151

    Staying Calm 152

    Short Cuts 153

PART 14: MEET CRAIG ALEXANDER RATTRAY. 156

PART 15: WHAT OUR ENTREPRENEURS SAY 158

PART 16: THE KNOW YOUR NUMBERS FRAMEWORK 162

PART 17: FINAL THOUGHTS FROM THE ROCKING CHAIR 164

PART 1: ROCKING CHAIR INTRODUCTION

NOTES

A rocking chair. What is the first thought that springs to mind when you think of a rocking chair? For me it's an old man or an old woman giving advice, and whilst I don't think of myself as either old or wise these themes and short stories are based on my weekly Friday afternoon videos from the rocking chair in my back garden where I share my thoughts, insights and things that have happened to me, and to my clients that week. I post them on LinkedIn.

I qualified as a Scottish Chartered Accountant in 1994 so I have been doing this for a long time and have worked with a variety of owner managed businesses and family-owned businesses for almost 30 years.

My focus is working with ambitious growing businesses and helping them grow and deal with the many and varied challenges along the way. Whilst my role is usually focused on finance it is all encompassing with respect to the business and the people, so I have an interesting perspective on these businesses and what makes them tick and what causes them problems.

Whilst I need to know the numbers and want you to as well, especially the key numbers, there is more to business than just that.

I see all sides of business and all sides of relationships. The good and the bad, the happy and the sad, the well performing and the struggling, success, and failure, the honest and the dishonest, and the givers and the takers. I've also seen marriage, divorce, birth, and death.

As business owners we must deal with all these things and our personal relationships at the same time as running and managing a business. There are different challenges every day.

Many of the large corporates do not understand this as it is very different to their business model.

I believe that business is about people and cash, and if you get both things right you won't go far wrong.

If you have the right people and you treat people well whether that is employees, customers, suppliers or funders and investors, and have the right financing in place you are likely to go far – assuming you have a commercial profitable business.

Business is personal. It is about people.

I like to approach business and life in general based on love, trust and helping people, and giving people the benefit of the doubt.

The purpose of this book is to help business owners on this journey as I know that owning a business is not easy. It is a rollercoaster and full of peaks (hopefully) and troughs (hopefully less so). The daily struggles and challenges of balancing a multitude of demands is never easy.

My thanks to my good friends Jeff and Stephen who have worked with me over the last few years and encouraged and assisted in making this book a reality.

These short musings at the end of the week are there to help people and I encourage you to read through them in your own time - take them, share them, and reflect them back on yourself.

Remember though – you are not alone and the challenges you are facing are being faced by many others just like you, and the many who have come through these challenges successfully.

I have categorised my thoughts through Parts 2 through 13, and if you take the first letter of each section it spells "ENTREPRENEUR" – you!

I hope you enjoy my musings.

To your success!

Craig Alexander Rattray

https://craigalexanderrattray.com

Welcome!

Welcome to "Rocking Chair Wisdom", a journey through the multifaceted world of entrepreneurship. In this book, we delve into twelve crucial themes, each a vital piece of the entrepreneurial puzzle. These themes, encapsulated in the mnemonic "ENTREPRENEUR," offer insights into Economic Strategy, Networking, Tenacity, Resilience, Education, Profitability, Rejuvenation, Ethics, Navigation, Empowerment, Understanding, and Resourcefulness. As you navigate through these pages, you'll discover not just the challenges and rewards of entrepreneurship but also the personal growth and learning that come with this journey. Let's embark on this exploration together, unravelling the complexities and celebrating the triumphs of the entrepreneurial spirit.

Every section of this book has self-reflection questions to guide you further on your entrepreneurial journey.

What part of this resonates with you?

_____
_____
_____
_____
_____
_____
_____
_____

Lessons From the Rocking Chair

Why do you want to continue reading this book?

_____
_____
_____
_____
_____
_____
_____

When you put your head on your pillow, do your business results help you sleep soundly?

_____
_____
_____
_____
_____
_____
_____
_____

NOTES

PART 2: ECONOMICS OF BUSINESS

In this section, we explore how strategic planning and economic acumen lay the groundwork for business success. Understand the nuances of market dynamics and how to position your business for growth and profitability.

NOTES

Understanding the Working Capital Cycle

One of the big challenges that growing businesses face is cash and "understanding the working capital cycle."

We raised £250,000 for a company that is sitting on a lot of surplus cash already.

We want to build a war chest for the things that we are looking to do going forward.

We have put in place a working capital facility of £1,000,000 for another client who is growing rapidly. They are bringing on new people and doing new things.

I am sure you have heard the old saying about fixing a roof, when it is sunny, rather than waiting for the rain. This is a good way to look at cash as well, making sure that you have got it there in advance of you needing it.

I know that this is not always possible. You must make sure you have the right information for the funder. There are certain times where you want to make sure you get to the end of the year, you want the forecasts updated, or you want to find a big contract or some other work. Funding is about getting that timing correct.

But you should be able to see that, and you should be able to see further out when you need to do things if you are managing your cash and working capital on a regular basis. My clients all focus on managing working capital through a rolling weekly cash flow forecast.

The whole point of the rolling weekly cash flow forecast is it gives you the opportunity and the time to do things earlier.

I have a number of those meetings on a Monday and Tuesday with clients so that we can see that everything ahead is fine. Or if it's not, we do something about it.

For me, that is the big insight because cash is always at the forefront of the mind of business owners, whether you have lots of cash or not.

I have a couple of clients who are sitting on lots of cash now. They are in a very fortunate position that is helping us to grow the business and not worry too much about what may or may not happen.

My insight is all about cash, focus on it, manage it, stay on top of it and make sure you've got more than enough.

Do you have the working capital you need to grow your business?

What could you do differently if you had more working capital?

Delivering Value

Do you think about value and delivering value for clients? I do, a lot! We always want our clients to feel like they are getting value out of what they are doing with us.

For me, it is not just about the time that you spend and commit to clients. It is about what you do for them during that time.

The way I like to approach things as well are the results of getting things done, not how long it takes. I really don't care how long it takes when people do things. It is far more important to me that we end up with the result that we are looking for.

That is a big thing that my clients look for as well. I like to deliver really good value for my clients.

This reminds me of a story that Roger Jones shared with me. My apologies to Roger in advance for this because I will not do justice to the story the way Roger does it.

Roger shares the story of a large cargo ship carrying millions of pounds of product. The ship was stuck in port because it had broken down. All sorts of experts had been looking at the problems over the course of a couple of weeks and no one could find the real problem.

One person suggested that there was a man named John who had experience with ships. John was an engineer. They had tried everything else, so they brought John in for his advice. John showed up. He was an old gentleman, probably in his 80s and very dishevelled. He had a long unkempt beard, and he boards the ship carrying a rucksack over his shoulder.

John shuffled slowly onto the ship towards the captain. John immediately asks the captain to take him to the engine room. John wanders around the engine room and he looks at the different controls and machines.

After a short while, John asks the captain to hand him his rucksack. The captain obliges.

John goes into the rucksack, and he pulls out a hammer. John taps a piece of machinery a single time with his hammer. He then tells the captain to see if the ship is now operable. To their surprise, the ship is fixed! Everyone is excited.

The captain says to John, "Thank you so much for your help. You have saved us so much time and money. Our investors are going to be really pleased. Please send me an invoice when you get home."

The next day, the invoice arrives, and it simply says, "Services for fixing the ship £10,000."

The captain looks at the invoice and thinks to himself that John was barely on the ship for 10 minutes, The captain went back to John and asked him for a detailed invoice.

John updates the invoice and sends it back. The total for the invoice is still £10,000 pounds, but there is more detail this time. The detail says "Fee for time on the ship £10 pounds, Knowing where to hit with the hammer £9,990. Total £10,000."

The key message is your clients care about the value that you provide, not about the time you spend fixing something. All of John's years of experience allowed him to know where to tap with the hammer. He delivered value for that Captain, whether he was on the ship for one minute, ten minutes, or ten days. It didn't matter because the captain got the result he was looking for and John delivered value.

Think about value going forward and think about surrounding yourself with people who deliver value for you.

Reflect on your approach to delivering value to clients. How do you prioritise the quality of results over the time spent on a task? Are there areas in your work where you could enhance value delivery?

Consider a situation where the focus is shifted from the time spent to the actual results achieved. How does this perspective align with your current practices? Can you

Lessons From the Rocking Chair

recall instances where the value delivered was more significant than the time invested?

Reflect on the story of John and the cargo ship. How can this story influence your perception of delivering value in your professional life? Are there lessons you can draw from John's approach that could enhance the way you provide value to your clients?

Reflect on a specific project or task you've worked on recently. How did the emphasis on delivering value, as opposed to focusing solely on time spent, impact your approach and the outcome of the project?

How might you consider the lessons learned and how you can apply them to future endeavours to enhance the value you provide to your clients or stakeholders?

EBITDA

I have had at least eight discussions with my clients about EBITDA in the last week. EBITDA stands for Earnings Before Interest Taxes Depreciation and Amortisation. These discussions are common and very important.

I believe that every single business owner or manager should understand the concept of EBITDA. And, I will have these conversations over and over until I am one hundred percent confident that my clients understand it.

Please go to the Know Your Numbers website (https://knowyournumbers.biz/where-have-you-been) and watch the EBITDA Video (about 2:40 in length). I ask my clients to watch the video over and over until they get a good understanding of the concept and what EBITDA is.

Give me a shout (or book a call) if you need any more help understanding EBITDA.

EBITDA is an important metric because that is how most businesses are valued by third parties. EBITDA shows the cash profit that has been generated within the business because we strip out interest, taxes, depreciation, and amortisation.

I also have clients who are looking to acquire businesses. EBITDA determines what we are willing to pay for the new business. To have those discussions with my clients who are looking at offers for the business or for part of the business, everyone needs to really understand what EBITDA is.

Do you understand the importance of EBITDA?

Reflect on your current understanding of EBITDA. How familiar are you with this concept, and do you feel confident in your ability to explain it to others? If not, what steps can you take to enhance your comprehension of EBITDA?

Consider the role of EBITDA in business valuation. How might a strong grasp of EBITDA positively impact the perceived value of your business by third parties? Are there specific actions you can take to leverage EBITDA for better business valuation?

Explore your business goals, especially if you are considering acquisitions. How does EBITDA play a role in determining what you are willing to pay for a new business? If you haven't yet delved into these considerations, what steps can you take to integrate

EBITDA discussions into your strategic planning for business growth or acquisition?

After watching the EBITDA video on the Know Your Numbers website, consider how EBITDA stripping out interest, taxes, depreciation, and amortisation impacts your understanding of your business cash profit. In what ways do you think this insight can inform your financial decision-making, and are there specific areas within your business where a focus on EBITDA could lead to strategic improvements?

Working Capital

I have a lot of conversations with my client about working capital. We also have working capital reviews with existing funders.

When my clients know their numbers, it is fun to see that their limits are going up. This is great news because it shows that the business is growing.

We have both a happy funder and a happy client. As one of my clients said, "there is no price that I can put on having a happy wife, and an unstressed life as a result of having this working capital facility."

Happy wife, happy life, right?

Actively and properly managing working capital is key in terms of growing your business. Managing working capital is also great for cutting out the stress that you have in your life.

You can have more peace, when managing your working capital is allowing you to make payments on time and to pay yourself properly.

Managing working capital is well worth doing.

How do you do it now?

How do you get working capital in place?

Well, first you must Know Your Numbers. There is no shortcut here. You must have good historical information and a solid forecast. You need to have detailed analysis for at least a year showing where you have been, and you need to be able to forecast where you are going.

It is simple once you Know Your Numbers.

I can guarantee that you will get funding if you can show detailed information to any funder. You must prove that you have an effective business model, the business is profitable, and hopefully you are building strategic value as well.

You will get funded every time if you can show those things to funders. Once you get a working capital facility in place, it is very easy to get increases.

As I said, we are working on a couple of increases now. I am working on increases and a couple of other overdraft facilities.

I have a new client that I took on in the last few weeks. We are working on forecasts where the business is probably going to grow from between two and ten million in new revenues. We have a great opportunity, and my role is to make sure we receive the funding to make it happen. This one opportunity will completely transform the business. It will be worth significantly more than it was when we started.

Think about your working capital facilities. Are you in a situation where all the cash comes in from your customers and it goes out the same day or are you able to plan?

Are you able to work out what you have in the bank, and you are not always scraping the bottom of the barrel, as they say?

Reflect on your current approach to managing working capital in your business. How do you currently handle working capital, and what strategies do you employ to ensure smooth cash flow management? Are there specific challenges or successes you've experienced in this aspect of your business?

Consider the importance of Knowing Your Numbers in obtaining working capital. How well do you know your financial numbers, both historically and in terms of future forecasts? What steps can you take to ensure you have detailed and accurate information that would support your case when seeking funding for working capital?

Explore the impact of effective working capital management on your overall business and personal stress levels. How has actively managing working capital contributed to a more peaceful business environment for you? What adjustments or improvements can you make to enhance the efficiency of your working capital management and reduce stress associated with cash flow challenges?

Consider the connection between successful working capital management and business growth. How have you seen working capital positively influence business expansion in your experience? If you haven't actively explored this connection, what steps can you take to leverage working capital for the growth and transformation of your business?

Growth

Here, I am discussing personal growth, as well as business growth. In many cases, it is personal growth that propels our business forward.

I observe this frequently with many individuals. They focus on personal growth, and subsequently, their businesses experience remarkable expansion. I can cite three or four companies that I am presently working with where the owners are doing that. As a result, I witness significant business growth. I facilitate their progress by ensuring they have the appropriate structures in place—effective processes, the right personnel, proper funding, and a thorough understanding of their financials.

In a recent scenario with a client, their turnover went from just over a million pounds in the year ending March 2021 to over 2 million pounds in the year ending March 2022. While the budget focuses on gross margin and EBITDA, securing orders exceeding £1.1 million in the first 21 days of this month illustrates substantial growth. This growth is attributed to the development of individuals within the team and the addition of an advisory board. The business, which initially had a monthly turnover of around £30,000 in 2020, has now grown to turning over around £500,000 a month.

Growth is achievable, but it requires understanding how to develop personally, making necessary changes, and implementing corresponding changes in your business. To capitalise on growth opportunities, having the right financial information and funding is crucial.

So, contemplate growth over the weekend, both for yourself and your business.

Reflect on a recent experience where personal growth positively influenced your professional life. How did it impact your business or work environment?

Consider the changes you've made in yourself that contributed to your business growth. What specific actions or mindset shifts played a significant role?

In what ways do you currently prioritise personal development, and how do you envision it further influencing your business growth in the future?

Measuring Performance

How do you know you have had a good day, a good week, a good month? Do you rely on instinct? Do you simply have a gut feel about how the business has gone? Whether the phone's been ringing, or you've been busy on-site, how can you prove it to yourself from a financial position?

This is something I have been speaking about this week in a Know Your Numbers Mastery Session. We were discussing KPIs and having different KPIs that allow you to measure and manage things, to track them. Some are generally strategic, while others are financial or operational. It's something you've got to keep measuring, keep in mind, and manage to improve your performance.

It's a key question for me—to move away from gut instinct to information. Base how you've had a good day, a good week, or a good month on facts and information generated from your financial or operational system. This means you can stop guessing, put it in place, and make a huge difference to your business. An absolutely huge difference.

Reflect on how you currently measure success in your personal or professional life. Is it based on gut instinct or information? How might incorporating more concrete data enhance your ability to assess and improve your performance?

Consider the key performance indicators (KPIs) that are relevant to your goals or endeavours. How regularly do you track and manage these indicators? What adjustments can you make to ensure a more strategic and informed approach to measuring your performance?

Explore the impact of weather or external factors on your well-being and productivity. How do such elements influence your daily routines and decision-making? What strategies can you implement to navigate and mitigate these influences effectively?

Where You Are, Where You Have Been, and Where You Are Going

I make sure that every one of my clients knows where they are, where they have been, and where they are going. It's something I talk to my clients about all the time, ensuring we have the financial information that gives us the answers to all of that.

It is important to think about what you are doing in terms of your own life and your own business—where you are, where you have been, and where you are going.

I've been reflecting on this over the last week or so myself, taking a few days in the sunshine to reflect and plan. It gave me an opportunity to think about what I have achieved this year, what I am looking to achieve next year, and going forward. I am also working on a second book, following the completion of my first book, and I've made good progress over the last few days. The plan is to get it done in quarter one next year.

Just think about your own journey. Don't beat yourself up too much, and don't compare yourself to anyone else. Compare yourself to yourself—where you were previously, where you are now, and where you are going.

Reflect on your personal and professional journey over the past year. What achievements are you proud of, and what lessons have you learned? How do these insights shape your goals for the upcoming year?

Consider the concept of self-comparison mentioned in the text. How often do you find yourself comparing your journey to others? What impact does this comparison have on your motivation and well-being?

Explore your plans and aspirations for the coming year. What specific goals do you want to achieve, and what steps can you take to ensure progress? How does reflecting on your past and present inform your future?

Differentiation

I have been discussing differentiation extensively with my clients and in the Know Your Numbers groups over the last few weeks. For me, differentiation is key. It allows you to set your own pricing, avoiding direct competition, as what you're offering is distinct from others.

In a market where businesses are often reduced to a price war, differentiation is the game-changer. Instead of trying to be the cheapest, I encourage my clients to differentiate by providing something unique, offering superior quality, delivering exceptional service, or having a feature that sets them apart. This approach ensures that clients keep coming back because what you provide is not easily obtainable elsewhere.

Differentiation is not only about standing out but also has practical benefits. It allows you to improve your profit margins, enhance cash flow, and ultimately builds a more valuable business. If you lack a differentiated product or service, I encourage you to explore ways to set yourself apart. It could be in the way you deliver, the quality you maintain, or an exclusive offering that others don't have.

Avoid the race to the bottom in terms of pricing. Instead, focus on differentiation, and you'll find yourself on a path to a much more successful and sustainable business.

Reflect on your own business or professional offerings. Are there unique aspects that set you apart from competitors? If not, what are some areas where you could introduce differentiation?

Consider a situation where you or a business you know successfully differentiated itself. How did this impact its market position, customer loyalty, and overall success?

If you are in a market where price competition is intense, brainstorm ideas on how you can differentiate without solely relying on price. What value can you add or what unique features can you introduce to stand out?

NOTES

NOTES

PART 3: NETWORKING AND RELATIONSHIPS

Discover the power of relationships in this chapter. Networking goes beyond making connections; it's about building meaningful, mutually beneficial relationships that support your business and personal growth.

NOTES

Opportunities

Let's talk about opportunity, or more accurately opportunities. One of the things that I encourage my clients to do is focus on the abundance mindset.

There are lots of opportunities out there. Unfortunately, most people don't really think about them because they don't believe that they have the funding that they need to allow them to deliver those opportunities.

I like to approach on the basis that funding is unlimited. I say that there is a pot of money over in the corner. You can take out of that pot whatever you want. To be clear, you must pay for it, the money is not free.

Next, you work out what you would do with the money if you decided to take it. With my clients, we build a plan that shows what we will do with the funds. We then go and raise that money to allow us to fund our plans for growth.

I have four or five different funding opportunities that we have kicked off this week. My clients have seen the opportunities that they can go and attack and they can go and deliver.

What we are now doing is funding their plans for growth. This is fantastic and it is exciting.

I encourage you all to think "What opportunities are there that you perhaps think you can't do yet?" We love to turn the impossible into possible.

What are the opportunities that you are not even thinking about?

Are you limiting your approach because you don't think you can get things funded?

In my Know Your Numbers groups, we focus on changing the way people think about their business numbers. More importantly, you take that knowledge and then apply it in your business. What you do with that knowledge will create opportunities for you as well.

What opportunities would you pursue if you knew you couldn't fail?

What would you need to do differently to be confident that you wouldn't fail?

How might you find funding if you knew you could succeed with a new opportunity?

Keeping Funders Close

Keeping funders close is something that I have spoken about many times. I encourage my clients to make sure that they let the funders know what is happening in their business. You tell them everything, share everything, work with them, have them round a table with you.

Sometimes clients don't like that. A reasonably new client from probably about three months or so wasn't particularly keen on that and had a distant relationship with the bank. The bank had declined some things during Covid, and I've been encouraging them to embrace working together.

We had a meeting yesterday with three people from the bank. We shared a presentation regarding where we were, where we are, where we are going, and various other things happening in the business. They were delighted to see the transparency and delighted to be taking the time to do it. It just went fantastically well.

As a result, the bank is now saying, "we can do this, and we can do that, and we can do that," and they will come up with some different ideas. Absolutely fantastic. We will continue to work on that relationship, continue to share information and have regular meetings, and I'm very confident that the bank will support the business going forward.

This isn't a business that's been around just for a short period of time. This is a business that's turning over 20 million pounds and will do significantly more next year. So, we need the bank to support us, and the way to do that is to keep them close, tell them where you've been, where you're going, something I keep saying and will keep saying.

Reflect on a time when sharing detailed information about your business with funders or stakeholders led to positive outcomes. What lessons did you learn from that experience?

Consider the importance of maintaining a transparent relationship with your financial partners. How do you currently communicate with your funders, and in what ways can you enhance this communication to build a stronger relationship?

Imagine a scenario where you're presenting your business status and future to funders. What key information would you share, and how might this contribute to their understanding and support?

Relationships

I have been thinking a lot about relationships over the last few weeks, given some of my travels and the occurrences. I have come to realise the importance of relationships in both business and personal life—how connections deepen, and how you align with people who share your values and ambitions.

Recently, I had a meeting with someone I hadn't caught up with for more than five years. Surprisingly, it felt like we had just met a few weeks ago. She operates on the same basis as me regarding dealing with people, fostering relationships with clients, and emphasising the significance of that over just completing a piece of work. This approach influences how I choose my clients. Admittedly, I've made a few errors in judgement towards the end of last year.

Reflecting on relationships extends beyond the professional realm to my personal and family life, including extended family. The importance of connections with those who resonate with your wavelength and can elevate you to a different level is evident. It's about dealing with people who contribute to growth and mutual support.

I hope that makes some sense today. On a personal note, my relationship with my little cat, Amadeus, is not as it was a couple of months ago. He's still very ill, and my apologies for missing last Friday. I couldn't really speak then. I appreciate the many phone calls and messages, expressing love and support for Amadeus. Hopefully, that positive energy will aid him in his long road to recovery.

Consider the reflections on relationships shared in the text. How do you prioritise and nurture relationships in both your personal and professional life? Are there specific experiences or encounters that have shaped your views on the importance of relationships?

Reflect on a past or current relationship that aligns with the theme discussed. How has this relationship influenced your personal or professional growth? In what ways have shared values and ambitions played a role in the connection?

Explore the challenges and nuances of choosing clients or partners. How do you navigate the decision-making process in forming professional relationships? What criteria do you use, and how have past experiences influenced your approach to these decisions?

Support

I just had a good strategic meeting with a client for three hours off-site to get our minds aligned with where they were going on the bigger picture.

It got me thinking about support because I support various clients in terms of their strategic and financial roles. But then I look at myself and consider the support I have around me.

I've got support from a business coaching perspective non-exec side, which is great because I'm a one-man business. I don't really have anyone to talk to about these things, so it's great to be able to bounce ideas off someone. That really helps me.

I've got support from my Greek tutor in terms of my language learning.

In terms of other support, I have some marketing support and additional Know Your Numbers support from Stephen Arthur, who is doing a great job on all those fronts.

Other than that, I don't have a huge amount of support. I know how challenging it can be for people doing their own thing because it's challenging to run your own business, whether you're a one-man business or have 20 or 50 people.

It's great to have someone to bounce things off. I've done that with a couple of clients this week who have just sat over a coffee and discussed or debated where we're going over the next few years. It's amazing the insights that emerge when you take a step out from the normal environment and engage in these conversations. I highly recommend that.

Reflect on the support systems you currently have in your personal or professional life. How have these support networks contributed to your growth or well-being? Are there areas where you feel the need for additional support?

Consider a time when taking a step back from your usual environment led to valuable insights or solutions. What was the context, and how did the change of setting impact your perspective or decision-making?

If you're a business owner or working independently, think about the challenges you face in seeking support. Are there specific areas where having a support system could make a significant difference? How might you go about establishing or expanding your support network?

PART 4: TENACITY

Entrepreneurship demands grit and perseverance. This section delves into the importance of work ethic, discipline, and the relentless pursuit of your goals, even in the face of adversity.

NOTES

Time

Can we talk about time?

Many people use time, more precisely a lack of time, as an excuse for failure. I stopped using time as an excuse for things several years ago.

We use "time" as an excuse for not going to the gym or eating healthily and not doing other things. Our excuses have nothing to do with time.

It comes down to what is important to us. If something is important enough, we will prioritise it and make time for it.

You will make time to go to the gym if it's important to you to go to the gym.

You will make time to eat properly if it's important to you to eat properly.

I try my best not to use time as an excuse, I don't think about time. I do what is important to me. I will find the time for the activities that matter to me.

That might mean working out in the morning, in the afternoon, perhaps at 10 in the morning or 10 at night.

I have had several business owners contact me saying "I really like what you're doing with Know Your Numbers, but I don't have the time at the moment."

I would argue that business owners do not have the time to not know their numbers. I know that by joining the groups and maybe joining the one-hour clinic, that in just three hours in a month, you will get more than that back in terms of the value it gives to you and your business. That value might be in terms of better information, making sure you get better funding, or just actually reducing the stress. Reducing stress in your business might allow you to enjoy time with your friends and family on weekends rather than stressing and thinking about work.

Take the time to think about how you see time. Assuming you have the time is, is time that important? And is time something you are going to use as an excuse going forward.?

How might you be using "time" as an excuse in your life right now?

How would you use your time differently if something was critically important to you versus unimportant to you?

Time (after Time)

How do I have the time to do everything I'm doing? It's a good question. I just do. I get on with it. I have lots of client-related work that can pull me in various directions. I've had a couple of days with meetings running into calls and not much time. But I'm still managing to use the gym every day, work on my Greek lessons, and allocate between one and two hours to Greek every day. I just finished a lesson.

I don't have time to be ill. The focus for me is very much on getting things done and getting the right things done.

If you ask anybody who wants to keep growing and developing how they do it, they just do. When it's something you want to do, you make time for it.

Something I've learned over many years is that you just crack on and get it done. I'm conscious of everybody's time.

Reflect on a time when you felt overwhelmed by tasks and responsibilities. How did you prioritise and manage your time to ensure that important things got done? What strategies did you employ to stay focused and productive?

Consider the statement, "If it's something you want to do, you make time for it." Think about a goal or activity you've been putting off. How might this perspective influence your approach to making time for that goal or activity in your schedule?

Explore the concept of focusing on "getting the right things done." What criteria do you use to determine the importance and urgency of tasks or activities in your life? How can you ensure that you prioritise tasks that contribute to your overall growth and development?

Discipline

I have a lot of discipline in my personal life. I will get up early or work late if I need to get something done. And, if something is important to me, I make time to do it.

I am over fifty and people tell me often that I am in great shape. I work hard to keep myself in shape. That is all about discipline. Part of my daily routine is to get a good workout finished first thing in the morning, before I do anything else.

Most days, I am either lifting weights or spinning. For example, the other day, I was in the gym at 4 am for an upper body weight training session and I finished with a 30-minute spinning session. I went back for another workout that same afternoon. I do not do that every day, but the discipline keeps me fit.

I have discipline because I have created habits that support me. Just like me, you need to be disciplined in your business. You need to be disciplined and to create habits, particularly when it comes to financial management.

You should be up to date on your financial management every single day. Make sure your bookkeeper is doing your bank reconciliation every day. Make sure your bookkeeper processes your sales invoices and purchase invoices daily so that you can update your cash flow.

You will never fall behind if you do everything every day. Stay completely up to date and you will be able to monitor your progress.

Little disciplines and habits can have a big difference on your business. It is creating those disciplines and creating those habits that will change your business. They will also change your outlook and your business finances. Discipline will also change the profitability and the cash flows within your business.

Remember, you can't manage what you don't monitor. The discipline of monitoring your business every day will just create a better business for you. You will know exactly where you are, and you won't have to worry about things.

You won't ever think "I need to pay this bill next week, but I don't have the cash." You can rapidly improve your business by creating weekly meetings about cash flow as well as month end finance meetings and board meetings.

These disciplines will make all the difference in your business. For me, discipline starts with Knowing Your Numbers. You will be fine if you Know Your Numbers in all the important areas of your business.

You won't have to worry about anything. You will be relaxed, and you will feel much better. You will be so much more confident, and you will have a better business.

A little discipline can go a long way. How can discipline help you build your business right now?

Reflect on your personal habits and discipline in your daily routine. How do you prioritise important tasks and maintain discipline in your personal life? Are there specific habits or routines that contribute to your overall well-being and productivity?

Consider the analogy between personal discipline and business discipline. In what ways do you currently apply discipline to your business, especially in financial management? Are there daily habits you can establish to stay up to date on your financial information and monitor your business progress effectively?

Reflect on the impact of discipline on your business outlook and financial well-being. Have you experienced positive changes in profitability and cash flows by implementing discipline in your business practices? How can you enhance or establish disciplines such as regular cash flow meetings, month-end finance meetings, and board meetings to improve your business management?

Explore your current approach to monitoring your business. How often do you engage in financial meetings or discussions to assess cash flow, profitability, and overall business performance? If there's room for improvement, what specific steps can you take to incorporate more disciplined monitoring practices and create a better business environment?

Hard Work

Often, work can be hard. At the end of the day, we get out what we put in. I remember being told that, I think, when I was about three years old, by my father. Spend time doing things properly and work hard. It is something that has just been ingrained in me my whole life in everything I do.

I see lots of people out there who do work very hard. And I see all those people out there who do not work very hard. It is not just about working hard. It is about working on doing the right things, or working smart, as well as working hard. I have had lots of people commenting, there seems to have been some change in me over the last few months because I have been working hard in the gym. It has not been the result of any quick fixes or taking any pills or steroids. It is just working very hard. And it is the same in business.

I am now at this stage where I have been fortunate enough to be able to cut back on several things on one-to-one clients because I have so much happening. And that has come because of working hard. Now, we have had to work smart to do that as well. You ultimately must deliver something that people want, that people find valuable, and are prepared to invest in.

But for me, life is just about working hard to get where you want by doing the right things. And I do worry about the younger generation who seem to want things immediately without working too hard. And maybe that is me just being an old guy. No, but that is the way I feel. People want instant success. And you know, instant success only comes after many years of hard work in lots of cases.

So, my advice to anyone out there, like my father said to me, if you want anything, go out and work very hard to get it. Now at the same time, I like to add, work smart as well. Work hard AND work smart. Do not work too hard, be smart, and have some relaxation time.

Reflect on a significant accomplishment in your life that required hard work. How did this experience shape your understanding of effort and reward?

Consider a time when working smarter, not harder, brought you success. What strategies did you employ, and how did it change your approach to challenges?

Think about the advice given by my father. How do you balance the need for immediate results with the understanding that true success often requires long-term effort?

It is Not Easy

"It is not easy." I have had this discussion with a few people this week — business owners who are having some challenges. They are not all clients, but people I have been trying to help with various things. And I keep saying, if it were easy, there would be no employees as we would all be running our own business, because it is not easy. As an entrepreneur and a business owner, you have got a multitude of things to think about.

One of the things that causes problems all the time is cash — the availability of cash. And that is something that can easily be fixed. If you Know Your Numbers, you can get the right funding put in place. For me, that is really an easy one.

Another one people complain about a lot is people. It has been said that there are eight billion people on the planet, so you are just not looking hard enough. But it is clearly not as easy as that. And if you can find the right people, it certainly makes a huge difference to your business.

Because for me, business is all about people and cash. It is all about the relationships that you have, internally, externally, and how you operate them.

So, what if it is not easy? You have got to dig deep. Sometimes you are going to have some ups and downs. The journey of an entrepreneur is not a straight line; it is up and down. And my advice there is, do not get too high with the highs, do not get too low with the lows. Try and stay in a reasonably narrow band and you will get there.

If you keep doing the right things, if you keep looking after people, if you keep operating with honesty, integrity, and treating people properly, then you will have a good business.

Your business will do well if people want to deal with you. You will have an even better business if you Know Your Numbers, put the right funding in place, and you are not worried about cash. That will take away all the stress from both your business and your personal life.

Reflect on a challenge you faced in your professional or personal life that was not easy. How did you overcome it, and what lessons did you learn from that experience?

Consider the statement, "business is all about people and cash." In your experience or observation, how do successful businesses balance these two aspects, and what impact does this balance have on their success?

Lessons From the Rocking Chair

Think about the ups and downs of the entrepreneurial journey. How do you manage the emotional highs and lows, and what strategies help you maintain a steady course in times of fluctuation?

NOTES

PART 5: RESILIENCE

Learn how to navigate the highs and lows with resilience. This chapter focuses on managing stress, maintaining mental health, and developing the inner strength to overcome challenges.

NOTES

Breakthroughs

Breakthroughs can be very powerful. I have seen many situations where someone struggled and then had a breakthrough.

We have a lot of breakthroughs with our Know Your Numbers group participants.

We always start with a basic understanding of the basics of business, especially understanding your financial statements (profit and loss accounts, balance sheet, cash flows) and finance in general. Learning the basics often leads to breakthroughs because we didn't know what we didn't know.

I love the "aha" moment when my Know Your Numbers group members understand their financial situation for the first time. There is a real breakthrough moment when they manage to connect the information in their minds and begin to understand. They usually have another breakthrough moment when they manage to see how their new knowledge is relevant in their business.

Once they fully start to understand their own financial position, they see even more huge breakthroughs.

I like to ask clients "Can you remember when you sat in that seat six months ago? Can you remember what you were feeling and the things that were concerning you?" Then, "How do you feel now?"

It is amazing what we can do after a breakthrough, the impact is so massive.

We then take that breakthrough a step further in terms of where does that breakthrough take you going forward?

Think of yourself in another six or twelve months sitting in the same chair. What breakthroughs can happen over the next six to twelve months if we are focused on creating them?

The key thing about breakthroughs is that it is not just about having a breakthrough, it is about what you do after that. We focus on taking that learning, and then applying it to our next challenge. We are always doing the work in between the meetings because that's where people make the real breakthroughs. We point things out, then send our clients away to do the work on their own. We hold you accountable so that you reach your breakthroughs as quickly as possible.

Take a moment to think about the breakthroughs you have had in your past. What breakthroughs have you had? What breakthroughs would you like to have?

Reflect on your understanding of the basics of business, especially financial statements, and finance. Have you experienced breakthrough moments when learning these basics? How did this newfound knowledge contribute to your understanding of your business?

Consider the "aha" moments in your professional journey. When was the last time you had a breakthrough in understanding your financial position or relevant business concepts? How did this breakthrough impact your decision-making and overall business strategy?

Explore the concept of breakthroughs in your personal and professional development. Think about past breakthroughs and their impact. Looking ahead, what breakthroughs would you like to achieve in the next six to twelve months,

Lessons From the Rocking Chair

and how can you actively work towards creating and sustaining them?

Pain

I have suffered quite a lot of pain physically because of my back. I have been hospitalised for it for the first time ever. I have had some form of back pain for over thirty years, but I have never had such pain as I had recently.

My back pain has me thinking about people in business who are in pain regularly. Lots of business owners are in pain because they don't know their numbers. I meet many business owners who don't understand where they are financially, they don't understand where they are going financially, and they don't have the right funding in their business. Because of these three issues, they continue to suffer pain in their business.

I met my doctor and now I must take my medication, adopt a new customised exercise regime, and make some lifestyle changes. Assuming I follow my doctor's advice, this should take away my back pain.

Back to your business, if you can understand where you are, where you have been and where you are going, you will take away the pain of the unknown from your financial situation. You will be able to put in place the right funding for your business and you will take away all that pain.

I meet a lot of potential clients who are in massive pain from their business. I love seeing my clients go from pain to wellness once they Know Their Numbers. Now, they have certainty, clarity, and visibility in their business. Now, they can get the funding they need and are able to go forward without pain.

I can safely say that across all those clients that I have been working with over the last number of months, they all have greater confidence and less pain because they Know Their Numbers. All of them will say that their pain has gone away.

Reflect on your current financial situation in your business. Do you feel a sense of pain or uncertainty regarding your numbers, not knowing where you are financially or where you are headed? What specific challenges or concerns do you face in this aspect of your business?

Consider the analogy between managing back pain and managing business pain. How can understanding your financial position, history, and future, alleviate the pain of uncertainty in your business? Are there specific steps you can take to gain clarity and put the right funding in place for your business?

Think about instances where you have witnessed others in business pain. If you have experienced a transformation in your own business from pain to wellness by Knowing Your Numbers, what strategies or practices helped you achieve this shift? How can you apply these lessons to assist potential clients or colleagues who are currently in business pain?

Reflect on your experiences or observations of businesses transitioning from pain to wellness after gaining a deeper understanding of their financial numbers. What specific changes in mindset, practices, or strategic decisions played a pivotal role in this transformation? How can you incorporate similar approaches to alleviate pain and bring about wellness in your own business or those you work with?

Cash Flow Pain

I want to talk about the pain caused by cash flow and not Knowing Your Numbers or not being on top of them, or not making them a priority in your business.

Let's look at clients I've been working with for one year, two years, three years. When they first came to me, they were in pain. They had opportunities, but they couldn't touch them because they didn't have the right information or the right funding.

Fast forward, the businesses are romping ahead. Some of them are three, four, or five times the level of turnover that they were when I started with them. Profitability is significantly higher, shareholder value has fantastically increased, and the businesses are worth a lot more now. It's all because they made financing and cash a priority in their business.

I read an article earlier today that says more than a third of medium-sized companies in Scotland are worried about cash. Now, there's no reason to be worried about cash if you've got the right information. I keep saying it—if you know who you are, where you've been, you can work on where you're going. You can forecast properly, have the right funding in place, and remove cash pain. I can guarantee that anyone who comes to me with cash pain, I can remove that cash pain. It won't necessarily be overnight, but it will happen.

I had a conversation with a business owner earlier today. We've been working together since May, June time, changing the whole financial infrastructure, changing the setup of how we run the business financially. We're about

80% of the way there, and the difference it's made for him is huge. We've got an invoice finance facility of just under a million pounds lined up to come into that business as well. That will transform what's happening. So, his pain is being removed because he has made financing and cash a priority.

I encourage you, if you have financial pain in your business, do something about it, make it a priority, and you can make it go away. The change it will make, not just to your business but to life in general, is huge.

Reflect on a time when financial pain was a challenge for your business. How did you address it, and what changes did you implement to alleviate the pain?

Consider the impact of prioritising cash flow and financial management in your business. How have such priorities contributed to growth, profitability, and increased shareholder value?

Imagine a scenario where you have successfully removed financial pain from your business. How does this transformation affect your overall outlook on your business and life?

Struggling

I've been struggling this week. It's probably not something anyone has ever heard me say. But I had a debacle in Athens with lost credit cards, stolen mobile, changed flights, cancelled flights, and then our 5-day trip turning into a 10-day trip. I must admit that the debacle basically knocked me off my stride.

It's funny; I was speaking to someone about it earlier in the week. Basically, I think the reason for that is that I had been knocked off my path. I work towards a plan, whether that's daily, weekly, monthly, or longer-term.

It's like being on a safari. You're driving along, and then suddenly, you go off the main road, and it is bang, bang, bang, crash, and you're all over the place. That's how I felt in the last week.

As a result of that, I've been struggling a lot with energy. I've struggled going to the gym, I've struggled with my eating, all sorts of things. I have managed to stay on track with work stuff, but everything else seems to be suffering. I guess it happens with a lot of people in business, particularly if you don't have a plan. You don't know how to respond to these things.

I had a board meeting earlier today, and one of the directors of the company was seeing what a difference I had made to her by having a plan, having a financial forecast because a few things had gone differently than what was planned over the course of the last couple of weeks. Because she had that plan and we had visibility in terms of the rolling cash flow and the longer term, she was perfectly relaxed. If we go back two years ago, she would have responded very differently.

I know how it feels, and as a result, I understand how it feels for people who don't have plans. If you don't have a plan in your business, then I guess you're going to struggle a lot more than people who do have a plan because when things change, you can easily update and adapt your plan to the changes.

I'm going to catch up on many things that are still to do, fix my phone and other bits and pieces, credit cards, and banks over the course of the weekend, and I will not be struggling next week.

Share an experience when unexpected challenges knocked you off your path. How did you initially react, and what strategies did you employ to regain your focus and composure?

Reflect on a time when having a plan or forecast significantly impacted your ability to navigate changes in your personal or professional life. How did having a plan contribute to a more relaxed and confident response?

Consider areas in your life or business where you might be struggling due to a lack of planning. What steps can you take to create a plan or update existing plans to better handle unexpected changes or challenges?

Change and Challenges

I visited Syntagma Square in Athens, and I could see the Greek Parliament too. It looked like the fountain behind me was on strike that day, having soaked everyone else and spouting water straight at them. The Greek population was in the middle of a general strike. This place was full of people yesterday; the streets were jam-packed. There were police vehicles all around us as people were protesting as part of the general strike.

I want to talk about change and challenges because most businesses go through them. It's not about avoiding financial hurdles, but about how you react to those changes and challenges. I faced various changes over the course of last week in terms of my flights and plans.

Yesterday, there was a challenge when I arrived at the airport. I also had a challenge when I lost my phone and credit cards last Saturday. It's not so much that these things happen; it's how you react to them. Honestly, I didn't get angry at all, which may surprise some people. I focused on what I could control, and in those situations, I wasn't in control. So, I laughed, smiled, made jokes about it, and just got on with it.

The same principle applies in business. You can choose to feel sorry for yourself when something doesn't go as planned, whether it's a delayed order, a lost order, or delayed payments. What matters is what you do about it.

We all face setbacks and challenges, but it's about responding and reacting to them, getting up, and starting again. As I often emphasise in the Know Your Numbers groups when discussing forecasting, a forecast is merely a series of assumptions based on what we know today. If those assumptions change, let's adjust the forecast and make it more realistic based on what we now know. It's about assessing the impact of those changes on the business going forward.

Reflect on a recent change or challenge you faced, whether in personal or professional life. How did you initially react to it, and how did your reaction impact the outcome?

Consider a situation where you lost control, like me losing my phone and credit cards. How did you cope with it, and what strategies did you employ to navigate through the challenge?

In your business or personal endeavours, how do you approach setbacks and challenges? Do you find yourself dwelling on the problem or taking proactive steps to overcome it?

Uncertainty

It is fair to say that we all need an element of uncertainty in our lives; otherwise, life would be very dull, very boring. If we knew everything that was going to happen, then there would just be nothing, nothing would be changing. However, when it comes to your business, I like to encourage my clients to have more certainty. Running a business that is uncertain is very difficult, challenging, and stressful.

You can create certainty in your business by having the right financial information. As I was saying yesterday in our Know Your Numbers group, if you Know Your Numbers, you will reduce that uncertainty. You will have a lot more clarity and visibility in your numbers. To do that, you need to know where you are, where you have been, and more importantly, where you are going.

You need to be doing these things daily. You need to make sure everything is processed daily. So, you are fully up to date with real-time information.

There are several things you can do every day to help with that certainty. And it makes life so much easier. You can do all of that; you can have the right funding in place. You can have your forecast, your weekly rolling cash flow forecast, your longer-term monthly cash flow forecast, and you will know exactly where you are going. Then, paying your suppliers at the end of next week and employee wages and salaries at the end of this month, next month, and the following month will just be so much easier.

Reflect on how you deal with uncertainty in your personal and professional life. What strategies have you found effective in managing the unknowns?

Consider the balance between certainty and uncertainty in life. How does having a certain degree of uncertainty contribute to the richness of your experiences?

Think about the role of financial information in reducing business uncertainty. How can being informed and proactive about finances contribute to a sense of control and direction in your business or personal finances?

Digging Deep

Sometimes we must dig deep in our personal lives and our business lives just to get things done, not just to get through things. At the end of the day, we all have challenges, we have all got lives outside work and business. Sometimes things do not go as planned. Sometimes there are all sorts of unexpected things, like relationship challenges, illness, and all sorts, and we have just got to go on with it. It really is as simple as that.

We can all sit and make excuses, because there is always an excuse not to do something. If you want to find one, you will easily find an excuse not to do something. And at times, you just must dig deep, whether it is to get a report done, like a forecast completed or a cash flow, or it could be in the gym.

I started another workout program a couple of weeks ago. I think one day, by the time this comes out, I will be about the eighteenth or nineteenth day. And I am having to dig deeper now because it is challenging me to do things that are quite difficult for someone at my age, but I am digging deep, I am getting on with it.

And it is the same in business. There are a lot of things I am having to deal with at the moment. There are a couple of challenges, a couple of interesting positive challenges, but having to dig deep to get them done and get on with them. It is the same with Know Your Numbers. We have got lots of different things happening. But again, digging deep, putting the effort in to get them done.

Reflect on a time when you had to dig deep in your personal or professional life to overcome a challenge. How did you find the strength to persevere, and what did you learn about yourself in the process?

Consider the concept of digging deep to avoid making excuses. How do you recognize when you are making excuses, and what strategies do you use to push through them?

Think about a current or upcoming challenge in your life. What steps can you take to prepare yourself mentally and physically to dig deep and successfully navigate this challenge?

PART 6: EDUCATION

A commitment to continuous learning is key to staying ahead. In this section, we discuss the value of education, personal development, and cultivating a growth mindset.

NOTES

Blossoming and Blooming

I have a cherry tree in my garden. It is beautiful when it is blossoming, blooming, and growing.

That is what business is like for me. It is fantastic to see my clients when their businesses are growing, starting to blossom and flourish because they Know Their Numbers.

I am working on about eight different financial plans for these companies because they are growing. They need more cash to fund the opportunities that they are exploring.

The great thing about that is because we have already got the existing financial information, and the forecasts, it is then very easy to engage with the funders.

We are going through that funding process. It is such a joy to work with people who are ambitious and who want to grow their businesses.

I have landed more new projects and ongoing clients are looking for more help from me.

In our Know Your Numbers groups, we focus on how clients can grow their businesses. We like to brainstorm to find, create, and enhance the many opportunities that are in front of my clients right now. We love to find the opportunities that we have not even been thinking about.

I keep saying to people, "don't let cash be a constraint in your business." I know that together we can get the opportunities funded.

Reflect on the growth of your business or projects. How do you envision your endeavours blossoming and flourishing in the way a cherry tree does when it's thriving? Are there specific strategies or practices you've adopted that contribute to this growth?

Consider your current financial plans and the need for additional cash to fund opportunities. What steps have you taken to ensure that your financial information is readily available, and your forecasts are in place? How has this preparation facilitated engagement with funders and supported the growth of your ventures?

Explore your attitude towards ambition and growth. In what ways do you align with the individuals described in the text who are ambitious and eager to expand their businesses? How can you adopt a similar mindset to attract new projects and ongoing clients, fostering a continuous cycle of growth?

Dreams

Our dream is to build a home in Crete one day. We've found the ideal plot, but it means I need to rob two banks rather than one. But that's okay; we can work towards that dream. On Wednesday, we got to see the plot, not just from land, but we got to see it from the sea. So, the owner of the company took us in the boat, and we could see exactly where we can walk down to swim in the sea and that's our dream.

This week, one of my clients has received an offer for his business, which will give him the initial seven figures he's looking for, with double that over the course of the next two years. So, three years, which is great. That will allow him to fulfil his dreams. I have various other clients who are working on certain things like building a home, owning a boat, or it's just a certain number, allowing them to do the things that they want. So, they're thinking about this sort of thing on a regular basis because too many of us get caught up in the day-to-day, and we don't think of the bigger picture. We don't think of the dream; we don't think of looking after the family.

I have two questions for you: What is your dream, and what are you doing about it?

Reflect on your personal dreams and aspirations. What is the most significant dream you currently have, and how do you envision achieving it?

Explore the impact of your dreams on your daily life. Are you actively taking steps toward realising your dreams, or are they often pushed aside by day-to-day routines?

Consider the balance between short-term responsibilities and long-term dreams. How can you integrate actions into your routine that align with your larger life goals?

Reflections

I've been thinking a lot over the last week on various things in terms of where I am personally and where I am as a business. I've been a bit up and down, which is unlike me. Maria has been away in Greece for six weeks, maybe even seven now.

So, lonely at home and a couple of challenges with two clients where I raised very good working capital facilities for them both. And both have reneged in terms of payment. The facilities, one was about a third of their turnover, one was about half of their turnover, great rates, great margins. And these people have just decided that they're going to ignore what we've agreed, and they won't pay. And that was really hurtful to me. It's having a huge impact on me this week.

Both people are reasonably prominent on LinkedIn as well. And I just think it's an awful way to do business. I don't get angry. I reflect and work out what I could have done better. Did I give too much? Did I open too much? Was I just too giving? And they've just been take, take, take, and people like that I feel sorry for. So, hold on, reflect on that. What did they do? Well, it means I'll just change slightly going forward. But I'm not changing my approach.

I have the most amazing clients who are keen, generous, grateful, and they appreciate what I do. They're not just clients; they're friends, and the help, the support, the testimonials, and just the things they've said over the last couple of months have been fantastic. And I really, really appreciate that. So, I want to find more of those people. I'm appreciative of feedback from Know Your Numbers, and some of the presentations I've given in the last couple of weeks as well.

So, in reflecting, I'm not going to let these two individuals get me down, regardless of how much money it costs me. And hopefully, they will look at themselves and realise that what they've done is not correct, that they should learn, reflect, and do the right thing going forward. And I look forward to working with more of the clients that I love working with.

Reflect on a challenging situation in your business or personal life. How do you typically respond to setbacks, and what strategies do you use for self-reflection and improvement?

Consider instances where you felt taken advantage of or hurt in your professional relationships. What lessons can you draw from these experiences, and how might you adjust your approach to prevent similar situations in the future?

Think about the positive aspects of your professional life. Identify clients or colleagues who have provided support, appreciation, and positive feedback. How can you attract more of these positive influences into your professional network?

Remembering

I have been thinking about a lot this week, in terms of where I have come from, going back to my childhood, my upbringing, going through university, and setting up the business. It has not been easy to get here; there has been a lot of hard work. I remember all those things—the first clients, people introducing me—I am very grateful for all of that. I remember saying at the start if somebody had given me £50, I would have given them a lift to Glasgow airport. At that early stage, you do almost anything. Perhaps I was exaggerating a wee bit too much, but that's what it's like. As you build up a successful business, you can become more selective.

So, I have been thinking a lot. As I mentioned in a previous rocking chair video, I have had a couple of issues with unscrupulous clients who have not fulfilled the contractual agreements we have, and they are dodging payments.

One of them has been a real disappointment this week. He clearly doesn't remember what I have done for him. He forgets the emails he sent me praising the fantastic job I've done and overlooks some online posts and videos where he talks about me, saying what a great guy I am and what a fantastic job I have done.

For me, remembering is crucial - remembering where you've been and not forgetting where you've come from. My upbringing is very important to me. For me, that's key—hard work and integrity have gotten me to this point. I won't let anyone change that, and I will not compromise my integrity at any point in time. Remember what you've been through, remember who has helped you, and remember why you do what you do. Give some thought to that today.

Reflect on a challenging moment in your journey where hard work and perseverance played a significant role. How did you overcome it, and what did you learn from the experience?

Consider a time when someone supported or helped you in your endeavours. How did their assistance impact your journey, and have you expressed your gratitude to them?

Explore the concept of integrity in your personal or professional life. Are there situations where you had to make tough decisions to uphold your principles? How did these decisions shape your character and path?

Ambition

Something that I make sure all my clients have is ambition because if they do not, I do not want to work with them. This holds true regardless of whether they are turning over 1 million, 10 million, or 50 million. If their plan is to do the same next year and the following year, then it is of no interest to me. I want to work with companies that are growing and ambitious. All my clients demonstrate this; otherwise, I would not be working with them. It is fantastic to see the changes in some of the businesses I am working with.

This week, in a board meeting with clients, they have doubled what they did last year already—we've doubled the turnover and are ahead in profitability as well. Another client phoned me yesterday to share that they have just won a £1.3 million project. Such accomplishments are fantastic, and I love working with people like that because it fills me with energy. They are full of energy too, and it just rubs off. These individuals are building teams, raising money, and doing what they need to do, which is what I enjoy.

It's amusing; I laugh when I hear football managers being interviewed. They've won three games in a row, are in fourth place, and the interviewer asks, "Where do you see yourself finishing at the end of the year?" Nine times out of ten, the response is, "We just want to finish as high as we can." This seems visionless to me. I believe you end up where you end up. I have clients working towards specific targets— £5 million, £10 million, £20 million, £50 million—in terms of turnover, profit numbers, or exit values. Setting these goals in place means you are not meandering aimlessly; you are working towards a defined target.

Reflect on your current level of ambition, whether in personal or professional pursuits. What are your goals, and how actively are you working towards them? How does ambition drive your actions and decisions?

Consider a time when you achieved a significant milestone or accomplishment. How did that experience make you feel, and how did it influence your motivation and energy levels moving forward?

Explore the concept of setting specific targets for yourself. What are your short-term and long-term goals? How do these goals provide direction and purpose to your actions, preventing you from meandering aimlessly?

Continuous Improvement

What is continuous improvement? It's funny; someone said to me last week, it doesn't matter what you do or who you do something for, wherever you take the business, you're always looking at taking it to the next stage, doing something more, just doing something that gets better.

There's a similar discussion we had in one of the Know Your Numbers Mastery groups this week. We were talking about forecasting and using forecasts to make people accountable, to measure performance, and basically to improve going forward. One of the entrepreneurs in the group mentioned that it's something we're working on all the time. We're continually trying to improve it and striving to make it better, trying to get better at forecasting, just trying to get better at what we do with it.

So, it's something that I think is important—business and personal as well. Continuous improvement. Stay focused on it.

Reflect on a recent instance where you actively pursued continuous improvement, either in your personal life or in a professional context. What were the specific actions you took, and what were the outcomes of these efforts?

Consider the importance of continuous improvement, as mentioned in the text. How do you prioritise and integrate this mindset into your daily life or work? Are there specific areas where you feel there is room for improvement?

Explore your approach to accountability and performance measurement, especially in relation to your goals. How do you use tools like forecasting to enhance accountability and measure performance? What adjustments can you make to further improve these processes in your endeavours?

Learning Greek

Is there anything that petrifies you? And if there is, how do you overcome that? I realised over the last few weeks that learning Greek petrified me. I've tried lots of different ways to do it myself, bought books and apps, and took courses and all sorts of things. It just didn't work for me. Deep down, I was petrified of not being able to do it, of being made to feel silly, of feeling as if I don't know what I'm doing, and essentially feeling like a five-year-old again.

The way I overcame that is I just got to the point where I needed to do something, and I jumped in, picked a tutor. I've taken two lessons a week; I've booked 40 lessons. It's been fantastic so far. I've been spending between one and two hours most days learning Greek as well. It got me thinking about business owners who are petrified of finance, putting it off for 5 years, 10 years, 20 years, sometimes more because they're petrified of looking silly.

One of the things that we've deliberately developed in Know Your Numbers is a forum that allows people not to feel silly. There are no silly questions; you can't say anything that will embarrass yourself or make someone look at you like you don't know what you're talking about. It's not that environment. It's exactly how I feel with my tutor—a very safe space for doing that. I'm loving it, seeing the changes, and the more I do, the more I want to do. I see the same things in Know Your Numbers Mastery groups where people are learning things and then applying them to their business. It's fantastic to watch. There's been some great feedback if you've seen any of my posts this week. Several polls with recommendations and general comments—it's great. We've got another group starting on Thursday as well. I'm looking forward to that, and we will be doing more groups as we go forward because I really want to help people overcome their fear of numbers.

Reflect on a fear or challenge you've faced recently. How did you approach overcoming it? What motivated you to act, and what steps did you take to tackle the fear or challenge?

Consider the significance of creating a safe space for learning. How do you foster an environment where you and others feel comfortable asking questions or seeking help without fear of judgement?

Explore the idea of continuous learning and its impact on personal and professional growth. Are there areas in your life or business where you've been hesitant to learn due to fear? What strategies can you implement to overcome this fear and embrace learning opportunities?

Attitude & Outlook

Do you think about your attitude and outlook? How many of you know someone who's grumpy, always complaining, and always finding something wrong? I'm sure most of you do. I can think of a few people. However, I no longer spend much time with any of them because I don't want to be surrounded by such negativity.

Jim Rohn once said, "You become the average of the five people that you surround yourself with," which is a profound point to consider. Think about optimists and pessimists—what's the difference? An optimist tends to have a more enjoyable life because of their positive outlook. On the other hand, a pessimist will mope around, constantly complaining about this and that.

For me, it's about maintaining a can-do attitude, getting on with things, being happy, and maintaining a positive demeanour. That's the way I like to operate, and those are the people I prefer to work with. It makes a significant difference in my life. If you find yourself surrounded by negative influences, it's crucial to reassess and perhaps distance yourself from them. It's a lesson I keep trying to impart, particularly to my mother, who tends to exude negative energy. At 77, she may never change, and as a result, I spend less time with her.

Consider the people who fill you with positive energy and surround yourself with them. I'm known for being generally calm, happy-go-lucky, and focused on getting things done. Surrounding yourself with similarly positive individuals can make a significant impact. If you find that your attitude needs adjustment, take some time to reflect on it over the weekend. My advice to you is to embrace change and foster a positive outlook.

Reflect on the people you surround yourself with regularly. Do they contribute positively or negatively to your attitude and outlook? Are there any changes you can make to enhance the positive influences in your life?

Think about a situation where your attitude had a noticeable impact on the outcome. How did a positive or negative outlook affect your approach and the ultimate result?

Consider times when you've consciously chosen to distance yourself from negative influences. How did that decision impact your overall well-being and attitude? What lessons did you learn from those experiences?

Action

Action is crucial in every aspect of life, whether it pertains to business or personal development. If you aspire to enhance yourself or your business, you must implement change because consistently repeating the same actions will yield the same results. Growth and improvement require a proactive approach.

Many individuals express dissatisfaction with their inability to expand their businesses or elevate their personal lives. The primary reason for this stagnation is often a reluctance to take different actions. My LinkedIn posts consistently conclude with the phrase "take action and drive success" because genuine progress is contingent on proactive steps.

Reflecting on my own business, particularly in the context of Know Your Numbers, I recognize the significance of action on various fronts. The success of this approach motivates me to extend its application to diverse areas through collaborations. Similarly, in my fitness journey at 53, where building muscle becomes more challenging, I acknowledge the necessity of working harder and taking action.

In your business, attending training events and seminars is beneficial, but the true catalyst for improvement lies in translating acquired knowledge into actionable steps. The Know Your Numbers process emphasises the connection between learning and implementation, highlighting the importance of putting knowledge into practice.

Remember, action is not just about attending events and acquiring knowledge; it's about actively applying what you learn. Only through such dedicated efforts can you witness genuine improvement in your business and personal endeavours. Take action, and may your endeavours be met with success.

Reflect on a recent situation where you felt the need for change or improvement, either in your personal life or business. What specific actions can you take to initiate that change?

Consider instances where you attended seminars or training events. Have you consistently implemented the knowledge acquired from these experiences into your business or personal life? If not, what barriers exist, and how can you overcome them?

Identify a specific goal in your business or personal development. What actionable steps can you outline to move closer to achieving that goal? How can you ensure consistent action over time?

Why?

Why do you do what you do? I was asked this question yesterday, and it's something I often contemplate. Ultimately, I do what I do because I thoroughly enjoy it.

Helping businesses grow and succeed, making a positive impact, and alleviating stress is the core motivation behind my work. While financial success is important, there's a bigger "why" for me.

Family plays a crucial role in my "why." Supporting my kids and grandkids is a significant driver. As I record this, I'm preparing to spend the weekend in Disneyland Paris with my grandkids, providing them with experiences and opportunities I didn't have in my youth. This family-oriented "why" is a powerful force for me.

Reflecting on my involvement in Know Your Numbers, the joy comes from educating people about financial aspects like P&L, balance sheets, and funding. Witnessing individuals implement what they've learned, seeing them act, and achieving positive outcomes is immensely rewarding. A recent video testimonial from a participant in one of our groups deeply moved me, reinforcing the impact and importance of my "why."

Consider your own "why." Why are you doing what you do? If there's misalignment between your actions and your desires, delve into the reasons behind it. Understanding your "why" can guide you toward a more fulfilling path.

Explore the driving force behind your actions. Why do you do what you do in your personal and professional life? Identify the core motivations that propel you forward.

Reflect on the impact you aim to make. How does your "why" contribute to the well-being of others, whether it's your family, colleagues, or community?

Consider any misalignments between your actions and your desires. If there's a gap, dig deeper into the reasons behind it. What changes can you make to bring your actions in line with your true motivations?

Uncomfortable

Do you know how to go from uncomfortable to comfortable? I've been feeling that way this week, in the last week, and the last few weeks because, as many of you will know, I am learning Greek. The Greek alphabet is very different from the English alphabet. I will do a different video on that at some point, explaining some of the nuances with it. I think one of the reasons I've put off learning it properly over the last seven years is because of that; I just felt uncomfortable.

What I've actually done is, I've connected it to my future because I want to live in Greece. I want to be able to spend time with people and speak Greek rather than relying on them speaking English. That's what's driven me to do that. I've gone through a whole phase; I've been uncomfortable because the alphabet is different. I'm not particularly good at languages has been another excuse. I do numbers! So, change the mindset; I've never done something about it until now. I'll have lesson number five with my tutor today. I can read the alphabet; I can write now. And I can understand lots more. It's fantastic. I'm getting a real buzz from it.

I understand the pain that a business owner feels, not understanding financials and not knowing the numbers because it's very similar to what I'm going through here. So, what I'd suggest to you if you're in that position is you connect to your future. What do you want your personal earnings to be in a year, two years, three years? What do you want your business to be worth in a year, two years, three years?

Think about that and connect to that and connect to how you will feel at that point in time knowing that you understand profit and loss accounts, balance sheet funding and how to increase the value of your business because it's made such a difference to me doing this.

Think about doing that yourself. Think about investing some time and energy into doing that. If I can help with anything, let me know. If you want to join Know Your Numbers, let me know. We launched another group on Thursday, which is fantastic. We'll be launching another group either next month or the following month. Not sure yet. We need to work out timings and my time.

I can highly recommend going from being uncomfortable to comfortable. You've got to do something about it. The more you can connect to your future self and really see yourself in the future, the more you will be able to accomplish that.

Reflect on a time when you felt uncomfortable about a new challenge or learning endeavour. What motivated you to overcome that discomfort? How did connecting it to your future goals influence your decision to act?

Consider your current financial understanding, especially if you're a business owner. What are your future financial goals, both personally and for your business? How might improving your financial literacy contribute to achieving those goals?

Explore the idea of connecting to your future self as a source of motivation. How does envisioning your future self, equipped with new skills or achievements, impact your willingness to tackle uncomfortable situations or challenges?

NOTES

PART 7: PROFITABILITY AND FINANCE

Financial management is critical for sustaining a business. This chapter sheds light on financial literacy, cash flow management, and strategies to ensure the financial health of your business.

NOTES

Paying Yourself More

Paying yourself more is all about people and cash. I have had a lot of discussions with business owners about how they can grow their businesses. They often ask me, "How do we take advantage of the opportunities? How do we get to work less hours and take home more money?"

The key to this is that we need the right people in the business. When we make sure that the business is properly funded and has enough cash (and working capital facilities), we can bring in the people we need to supplement the management team, the strategic team, and the operational team.

In most cases, that will mean the business owners end up working less hours. Funding will allow us to fill other gaps that need to be filled, take advantage of opportunities, and pay the business owner more money than they are currently receiving.

I had a recent meeting with a client. They generate over £10 million. One of the owners is probably the lowest paid person in the company and he is working well over 70 hours every week. That is just ridiculous, you shouldn't be working that hard, unable to pay yourself more money.

One of the things we are working on is looking at where we are in terms of the historic accounts, getting that fully up to date. The bean counters (accountants) have been letting them down. I tell my clients to only work with an accountant who is interested in helping and doing more proactive things (rather than being reactive).

With my clients we want to have a serious discussion and build a forecast so that we can see what the business is doing now and where it is going. We make sure that we build in the right salaries for the owners and plan for the new people we need to bring into that business.

Once we have the plan, we will go and fund the business. We know that our plan will take this company to turnover north of £20 million within the next six months or so.

We want to focus on getting the right people onto our team with the right funding. This also frees up your time.

For most business owners, the three things that they are generally stressed and worried about are people, cash, and time. These are all things that can be fixed if you have a plan in place.

Reflect on your current business structure and team composition. Do you believe you have the right people in key roles to propel your business growth? How has the presence or absence of the right team members affected your ability to seize opportunities and manage your time effectively?

Consider your approach to financial management, especially regarding historic accounts. Are you actively keeping these accounts up to date, and how has the involvement of your accountant impacted this process? Reflect on the proactive steps you can take to ensure sound financial planning aligned with your business goals.

Envision your ideal business scenario in terms of funding, team composition, and financial planning. What steps can you take to bring this vision to life? How would having the right people, proper funding, and a well-crafted financial plan alleviate stress about people, cash, and time in your business?

Funding

There are a lot of discussions going on with funders about funding because some of my current clients are growing at a crazy rate - it's staggering, some of the things that are happening.

One client turned over two and a half million pounds by the end of May. We're forecasting to do about seven million pounds this year and then forecasting to go to about thirteen million pounds next year. And that might sound unrealistic, pie in the sky, but it's not, because the work and the contracts are there. So, we're putting in place a facility at the moment where the company has been self-funded so far. We'll have a facility of just under a million pounds to get us through the next year, and I fully expect that facility will grow significantly.

We've got a couple of clients where their funding is increasing. One's doubled the facility from half a million to a million because of the growth that's happening there. And I'm in discussions with another one with three different funders who are fighting for their business.

I suppose the funniest thing that's happened over the course of the last few weeks was not particularly funny in that sense. There's a client who's been growing aggressively over this year, and I've been doing an initial project for them to get them some funding and delivered a facility. We turned over a million last year, and I managed to get them a half-million-pound facility on a non-disclosed basis, told them beforehand what the cost would be, and what the structure would be. Now they're saying it's too expensive, which I find strange. They've said they've got a couple of clients who are going to pay them weekly and will pay them within a couple of weeks, which is fantastic for now. But give it another three months or four months when things bite, and they don't have the cash. What then happens to this company?

It's a very short-sighted view, in my opinion. As I've said to people before, they can complain about what the cost of certain facilities are. You've got to look at the bigger picture. You've got to do two things: compare that against what it may cost to raise the same amount in equity and what that potentially is going to cost you over three to five years. You've just got to think about the bigger picture. What can you do with that money? If it costs you 10 grand, 20 grand, 50 grand, whatever that may be over the course of the year, what can you do by having, say, an extra half-million pounds in your business? What profitability will it generate?

For me, those two things are very short-sighted views. But I'm just advising, and all I can do is tell my clients what I think they should do, and it's ultimately up to them to make decisions. I know the guys who are increasing the facilities are going to do very, very well. Unfortunately, this company who isn't going to take out that offer will have some problems in the next few months.

Reflect on a time when you had to make a financial decision for your business. What factors did you consider, and what was the outcome?

Consider the importance of funding for business growth. How do you currently secure funding, and what strategies could you explore to enhance your financial resources?

Think about the long-term perspective in financial decision-making. How do short-term cost considerations align with your business's overall growth and profitability goals?

Health and Wealth

I focus a lot on health, wealth, happiness, and success. What do you view as success? Ideally, you would want to have health, wealth, and happiness. But if you had to choose one, which would it be? For me, it would be health, hands down. Without health, you're unlikely to have the wealth to be able to work, and you're unlikely to be happy as well. So, everything for me starts from health.

I've probably battered my body a bit over the last couple of months, really pushing it into submission, and I'm struggling a bit with man flu. I'm feeling better today, but still coughing, and spluttering a little bit. Health, for me, is the key because without it, you can't work, you can't do what you're trying to do.

Fortunately, because I have all three now, in terms of how I feel, I'm very happy. I'm happy because I love doing what I'm doing. I want to do more of it and to just keep enjoying all of that for many, many years. As long as I look after my health, that, for me, will be success and allow me to keep working and doing the things I want to do.

So, think about what success means to you. Consider what's most important: health, wealth, or happiness.

Reflect on a time when your health significantly impacted your ability to work or pursue your goals. How did this experience shape your priorities and perspective on success?

Consider the interconnection between health, wealth, and happiness in your life. How do these elements influence each other, and what steps can you take to maintain a balance among them?

Explore your definition of success. What are the key components that contribute to your sense of accomplishment and fulfilment? How do your current actions align with your vision of success?

PART 8: REJUVENATION

Balancing work with personal well-being is essential. Here, we talk about maintaining health and wellness, and how taking care of yourself is integral to your success.

NOTES

Freedom

Freedom includes freedom of your mind and freedom of your spirit. Freedom can make a massive difference to a business owner who understands and knows their numbers. Having a properly funded business brings us even more freedom.

Over the years, I have observed numerous business owners who are completely stressed because they do not understand their current situation. They do not have the right funding in place. They cannot pay suppliers, wages, and they cannot pay themselves.

What happens is that the rest of the employees go home at the end of the day, and they typically will forget about the business. However, with business owners, they go home and cannot switch off. They cannot forget about stresses from the office. This might cause arguments with their family. Many business owners are present physically with their family but not mentally present. We might not be present because cash struggles are going on and on in our mind about cash and pressure.

"What do we do? How do we pay our suppliers? How do we pay our wages?"

It is fantastic for me when I see clients that I work with who have transitioned from that position to a place where they have complete and utter freedom of their mind because they know their numbers, they have the funding in place, and they know the suppliers will be paid next week, at the end of the month, event at the end of the quarter— all of these things. They know the wages have been paid.

It has been fantastic. Over the course of the last few weeks, several of my clients have gone on holiday. They are not stressed whatsoever, either before they go or while they are away because they know that we are on top of the numbers.

They know we are on top of the cash. It makes such a huge difference. It has been great just hearing some of the feedback from them and receiving feedback from funders over the last couple of weeks and various things we have been working on.

If you have freedom, I know that you can have fantastic weekends. Speak to someone like me if you are one of those people who do not Know Your Numbers, who do not have a properly funded business. You might know that you need to change, but don't know where to start. Speak to me, speak to someone who can advise you and get you out of that position.

For the rest of you who are totally free, and your mind is clear, you can go away and have a fantastic weekend with your partner and your kids. Congratulations!

Reflect on your current understanding of your financial situation. Are there aspects that cause stress or uncertainty? What steps can you take to gain a clearer understanding of your numbers?

Consider your personal and family life in relation to your business. Do you find it challenging to switch off from work-related stresses when you're at home? How might addressing financial concerns positively impact your family relationships and your overall mental presence at home?

Imagine a scenario where your business is properly funded, and you have complete freedom of mind. What changes would you see in your daily life, both professionally and personally? How would this newfound freedom impact your ability to plan holidays and enjoy stress-free time away?

Sleeping Soundly

How many of you sleep soundly at night? How many of you don't? There's a lot of uncertainty around now, with rampant inflation, increasing prices, rising interest rates, and higher energy bills. If you don't have control of your numbers, you might be worrying quite a lot. Even some people who are on top of it are still rightfully concerned due to the element of uncertainty.

My advice here is straightforward, and its advice I give all the time. You need to Know Your Numbers and be on top of your cash. Plan for what's going to happen, have proper forecasts. To have proper forecasts, you need to know where you are and where you've been. It's very simple. Get your numbers up to date, create a proper forecast, and once you do, you can start running your business properly. Update your forecast every week, create a rolling weekly forecast, update your monthly forecast at the end of every month, review it, understand your variances, understand what's changing, and it will give you time to react. As a result, you won't be as stressed, and you'll sleep better at night. For me, that's the key.

How confident are you in your understanding of your business numbers and financial situation?

What steps can you take to improve your financial forecasting and planning?

Reflect on a time when financial uncertainty affected your sleep. How did you address it, and what could you do differently in the future?

Health

Health is something that I have been reflecting on a lot. Realising that none of us are invincible, a friend has ended up in the hospital, and there are others facing life-changing and potentially life-ending situations. It's not a good place to be. As far as I'm concerned, if you don't have your health, you don't have anything. You can have a great business, all the money in the world, but we often take our health for granted. We don't know when our time is up or when something might happen.

There are things going on in our bodies and minds that we're not always aware of. I'm particularly conscious of this due to my father's experience—he had a heart attack at 35 and a stroke a week later. So, I've always prioritised looking after my health, which is why I can become a bit obsessed at times with the gym, nutrition, and overall well-being.

Few of us, when on our deathbed, will wish we had taken less care of our health. Most will likely be thinking that they wished they had prioritised it more, with perhaps less emphasis on the material aspects of life. I'm not trying to be deep and meaningful today; it just puts things into perspective for me. If we all take better care of our health, it will be better for us and our families.

Let's not drink too much, eat in moderation, exercise, and take care of ourselves.

How do you prioritise your health in your daily life? Are there areas where you feel you could improve, and what steps could you take to enhance your overall well-being?

Reflect on a time when your health played a significant role in your life or someone close to you. How did it impact your perspective on the importance of health, and what changes, if any, did you make as a result?

Consider your long-term health goals and the steps you are currently taking to achieve them. Are there adjustments or new habits you could implement to further support your health and well-being?

Feeling Tired

Are you feeling tired? I can certainly relate because I've been feeling tired in various ways—physically, mentally, and emotionally. I've been drained and, to use a good old Scottish term, a wee bit "scunnered." I've also been a bit frustrated with LinkedIn, which is why I haven't posted all week. Dealing with algorithm changes and a lack of engagement can be disheartening.

It's been a challenging week overall. Dealing with lawyers, addressing old debts, and preparing for a court case have added to the fatigue. I've also navigated a challenging working capital facility.

In times like these, I listen to my mind and body. I try to take a step back, avoid pushing too hard in the gym, go to bed earlier, and get a bit more sleep. Hopefully, over the weekend, I'll start feeling better.

As for the weekend plans, I haven't figured them out yet because I'm too tired and fed up at this stage. However, I'll do something to improve my mood, mindset, and tiredness.

Reflect on a time when you felt physically, mentally, or emotionally drained. What were the contributing factors, and how did you cope with or overcome the fatigue?

Consider instances where external factors, like changes in algorithms or a lack of engagement, affected your motivation or mood, especially in professional or creative endeavours. How did you manage these challenges?

Explore your strategies for dealing with challenging weeks or periods. Do you have specific self-care routines or activities that help you recharge? How can you incorporate these into your routine more consistently?

PART 9: ETHICS

Upholding integrity and ethical practices are non-negotiable. This section emphasises the importance of ethical behaviour and doing the right thing in all business dealings.

NOTES

Do the Right Thing

I was feeling a bit grumpy about dealing with a court case. The case involves a client who clearly owes me money, refusing to pay and making various excuses. I have three similar situations, all quite frustrating, given the quality of work and service I provided.

I had a similar experience with a client this week, facing complaints about work valued at 30 or 40 grand, which turned out to be a minor defect costing two grand. I see this often with main contractors and subbies, dealing with unscrupulous individuals.

I'm grumpy because there's no need for it. Business is about relationships, and if you can't have the honesty and integrity to deal with people on that basis, it's a problem.

I'm facing challenges with two clients not honouring agreements. I emphasise the importance of honouring agreements in business. I'm currently working my notice period with three clients, disengaging properly and professionally. Treating people the right way is crucial.

I'll try not to be too grumpy over the weekend, depending on how tomorrow's court case goes. It's frustrating to deal with dishonesty.

Reflection on integrity: Reflect on a situation where you had to uphold your integrity or faced challenges due to someone else's lack of integrity. How did you handle it, and what did you learn from the experience?

Business ethics: Consider the ethical aspects of your business dealings. Are there specific principles or values you prioritise in your professional interactions? How do you navigate situations where others might compromise these principles?

Agreements and expectations: Review your approach to agreements and expectations in business. How do you ensure clarity and honour commitments? Have you faced challenges with clients or partners not adhering to agreements, and how did you handle it?

PART 10: NAVIGATION

Change is constant in business. Learn how to adapt and navigate through uncertainty with agility and strategic foresight in this chapter.

NOTES

Visibility

I talk about visibility a lot. I talk about visibility with existing clients and with my potential clients.

Generally, they are asking how they can have more visibility in their business. They ask me "How will working with you give me more visibility in my business? Will I have visibility if I work with you?"

You must have good financial information if you want to have good visibility in your business. Having good financial information is critical to better visibility.

In Know Your Numbers, we spend a lot of time going over where you are, where you have been, and most importantly, where you are going. By knowing the first two, we can work out where we are going. We can have forecasts in place, weekly rolling forecasts, monthly profit and loss, as well as balance sheet and cash flow forecasts. That allows us to manage the business much better. We can see where we are going and what resources we need to get there. We can see the cash requirement and we can secure the working capital facilities that are needed.

Visibility is what drives the business forward and allows us to take advantage of opportunities. You can take advantage of opportunities that you previously didn't think you could. For the business owner, it also means that you can pay yourself more because you have the funding in place to allow you to do that.

How are you ensuring that you have the visibility that you need in your business?

Reflect on the importance of visibility in your business. How has the concept of visibility been a focal point in your discussions with existing and potential clients? What specific questions or concerns have they raised regarding visibility, and how have you addressed them?

Consider the role of good financial information in achieving visibility. How do you currently manage and utilise financial data in your business? Are there areas where improvements can be made to enhance the quality and accessibility of your financial information for better visibility?

Explore your current practices in forecasting and planning for your business. In what ways do you assess where you are, where you have been, and where you are going? How can you implement or improve forecasting tools like weekly rolling forecasts, monthly profit and loss, balance sheet, and cash flow forecasts to enhance your business visibility and strategic decision-making?

Reflect on the impact of visibility on your business decisions. Can you recall a specific instance where having better visibility allowed you to seize an unexpected opportunity or navigate a challenge more effectively? How can you consistently ensure that visibility remains a priority in your ongoing business strategy and decision-making processes?

Juggling

It's been a tough week; I've been juggling many things. Towards the end of last week, something happened that required several meetings, and I've had to do an extra 20 hours of work on that specific thing, on top of everything else. Most of you who run businesses will be familiar with that because you're juggling every day.

What I've found over the last few weeks is that some of my very fast-growing clients have so many opportunities coming in—opportunities that exceed their entire turnover from last year. One of them is turning over a couple of million, and we'll likely double that to close to five. This means a real ramp-up in scale, and it's important to get the right people. As many business owners know, there are real challenges in getting people now.

Juggling becomes a part of business, but it's also part of our personal lives because most of us have families and other demands. We're juggling personal and business aspects, and it's just something that we need to do. I know if a client needs something from me, I'll do it; I just need to juggle things and work more hours. That's what happens, and it does become a bit of a skill.

Juggling, as we've all seen, going from three balls to four balls to 10, is challenging, but the more you practise, the better you get. So hopefully, you're not juggling too much this week, and you won't have to juggle too much at the weekend.

Reflect on a time when you had to juggle multiple tasks or responsibilities. How did you manage the situation, and what did you learn from the experience?

How do you prioritise tasks when faced with numerous opportunities or challenges in your business? What strategies do you use to maintain balance?

Consider the balance between personal and business life. Are there specific areas where you struggle to juggle

Lessons From the ROCKING Chair

responsibilities? What adjustments could you make to improve this balance?

Change

Change is imperative for growth and for steering our paths towards different destinations. There's a classic saying, "If you always do what you've always done, you'll end up in the same place." It emphasises that without change, nothing substantial will occur.

Over the past several months, I've implemented numerous changes, and in the recent weeks, I've altered the foundation of my collaboration with certain individuals. I've resigned from three clients as my business undergoes transformations, requiring more time for initiatives like Know Your Numbers. Change can be both exciting and bittersweet, especially when parting ways with clients. However, ensuring an amicable disengagement and offering ongoing support reflects the positive side of change.

In the Know Your Numbers Mastery groups, I've witnessed significant personal and business transformations.

Participants are making changes, absorbing knowledge from the groups, and applying it to foster growth in both themselves and their businesses. The feedback received in the past weeks has been truly inspiring.

I encourage each of you to contemplate change. If you're content with your current circumstances, that's perfectly fine; no change is needed. However, if you aspire for more, if you wish to find yourself in different places, embracing change is essential. Attending events, reading, and participating in seminars or webinars are steps in the right direction, but real change only occurs when you apply these learnings to your business.

As you implement change, growth becomes inevitable—both for you and your business.

Reflect on the recent changes you've made in your life or business. What motivated these changes, and what positive outcomes or challenges have you encountered?

Consider a situation where change is needed, either personally or professionally. What specific steps can you take to initiate this change? How do you envision this change contributing to your growth?

Think about a time when you resisted change. What were the reasons for your resistance, and what lessons did you learn from that experience? How can you approach change differently in the future?

Evolving

This section is more upbeat, and it's about evolving. We all evolve, and so do our businesses. For me, evolving is about changing and developing. In my own business, there are changes happening, developments occurring, and it's evolving. The work on Know Your Numbers and other projects is taking a different direction.

When I look at my clients, I see them evolving, developing, and growing. They're undertaking different initiatives, building teams, raising capital, and making more money. Evolution is a continuous process, and it's up to us to decide in which direction we want to go and how we manifest change.

Reflect on a recent change or development in your life or business. How did you adapt to it, and what positive outcomes resulted from the evolution?

Consider areas in your life where you feel the need for change or growth. How can you initiate the process of evolution in these areas? What steps can you take to move towards positive development?

Think about your attitude toward change. Do you generally embrace it, resist it, or feel indifferent? Explore how your perspective on change influences your personal and professional life.

Darkness

The question is, are you operating in the dark? Do you still not have visibility of your financial information, and as a result, authorised funding in your business? I've spoken to a few people this week on the back of some new videos that we're launching for Know Your Numbers with some testimonials from people. What's clear coming from those testimonials is the value that people are getting from knowing their numbers, understanding their business, the changes it's making to their business and to their life.

Given the very uncertain world that we're living in now, and the way things are changing at very short notice, you must be on top of your numbers. So, if you're still operating in the dark, fumbling around not properly understanding your numbers, you need to do something about it. Because this uncertainty is just going to make things worse for you.

The coming months aren't going to be difficult for those who aren't on top of the numbers. The people who have visibility also have clarity and certainty and with their forecasts they will be able to adapt to change. We've seen inflation moving significantly higher; we've seen interest rates go up. Who knows what's going to happen with them? Who knows what's going to happen with different projects people are working on? We don't know.

But if you've got a forecast, you can adapt to those changes very quickly.

I encourage all of you to stop operating in the dark. Try and get some visibility and light into your business. And for those who haven't done so yet, join one of my Know Your Numbers groups. Or if you want to have a chat about something, give me a call. Because the pain that you will cause yourself over this period without Knowing Your Numbers is going to be huge. And I know that you can change that pain quickly, as my clients have.

Reflect on your current level of financial visibility in your business. What areas are still in the dark, and how can you bring more clarity to your financial information?

Consider the impact of uncertainty on your business. How would having a clear understanding of your numbers help you adapt to unexpected changes or challenges?

Explore the steps you can take to improve your financial knowledge. Are there specific resources or groups, like the Know Your Numbers groups mentioned, that you can join to enhance your financial awareness?

NOTES

PART 11: EMPOWERMENT

Fostering a positive environment is empowering. This section discusses the power of positivity, gratitude, and building a supportive culture for yourself and others.

NOTES

Gratitude

I am going to share my thoughts on gratitude and the things for which I am grateful.

I recently celebrated my wedding anniversary. I am so grateful for having my lovely wife, Maria, in my life. Spending time with her is very much a priority for me. That doesn't always happen through the week, but we do make a lot of time for each other over the course of the weekend.

I am grateful for the fantastic life that I have built. I am grateful for my wonderful clients. I am loving every day.

I can't imagine waking up every day and going to work thinking "I don't want to do this. I don't want to do that." I genuinely love everything I do, which is why I work and work. I'm very grateful for what I do.

What are you grateful for?

What changes would you like to make in your life to have more things to be grateful about?

What will you be grateful to have changed in the next year when you look back?

More Gratitude

On the continuing topic of gratitude, I had a very special week with a visitor to Glasgow on Tuesday. It was a special time for me, and it got me thinking about how grateful I am for everything. I am happy, fit, and healthier than I have ever been. Mentally, I am very focused and switched on.

I am having such a great time working with my clients, who are fantastic. It's such a privilege to work with them.

They are ambitious, want to do things, and are also grateful. They express their gratitude to me. I've received lots of good comments over the last few weeks.

I've done a couple of interviews with people for the next Know Your Numbers release, and it's nice when people show that they are grateful for things you've done. In many cases, people forget what you've done for them yesterday, but now, I have to say I have the most amazing group of clients. I am just so grateful for that.

Everything is good with my family and my kids. I am heading off on holiday on Sunday, and again, I am very grateful for that. I have quite a lot of things to do before I go, but that's fine. I never complain about the work and the things I must do because it's just part of what I do, and I really enjoy it.

So, gratitude. Think about your own position. What are you grateful for? I'm sure when you put your mind to it, there are many things for which you will be grateful. I am also grateful for spending a week with my lovely wife because she's going to be in Greece probably for another six or so weeks after that. I'll be home alone again, but grateful for having opportunities to spend a week with her in Greece.

Reflect on a recent experience that made you feel grateful. How did this experience positively impact your well-being and outlook?

Consider the people around you, such as clients, family, or friends, for whom you are grateful. How do these relationships contribute to your sense of fulfilment and happiness?

Explore your attitude toward work and responsibilities. How can you cultivate gratitude for the opportunities and experiences that come with your professional and personal responsibilities?

Even More Gratitude

While I have talked about gratitude before, I believe one can never express gratitude too often. It's been a good week, with many positive developments. Generally, I'm grateful most days for what I have in terms of my life, my family, my business, and all the rest of it. However, this week has been exceptionally good.

I've received amazing feedback from interviews conducted with previous Know Your Numbers participants. There has been great feedback from funders I've been working with, and meeting people at an event last night was enlightening. The number of people who watch the rocking chair videos that I don't know about is incredible, and the feedback from them has been great as well. I'm feeling happy, positive, and very, very grateful.

The clients I'm working with are amazing. I've received recommendations for working with other people, and there are potential collaborations with Know Your Numbers. So, today, I'm feeling grateful. I'll keep it short because I need to go and finish my Greek homework, which I haven't done yet due to a very busy week. I wish you all a fantastic weekend. Take a moment to ponder what you're grateful for during your time off.

Reflect on the positive aspects of your week. What specific moments or achievements are you grateful for, and how do they contribute to your overall well-being?

Consider the people in your life who have provided support, feedback, or recommendations. How has their presence impacted your journey, and how can you express gratitude towards them?

Explore potential collaborations or opportunities that have arisen recently. How can you leverage these opportunities, and what steps can you take to further enhance your professional or personal growth?

Dreams into Reality

Can we talk about turning dreams into reality. Pluto is joining me today as a gift from my grandkids after our visit to Disney last week. Disney's theme is about making dreams come true. So, how do you turn your dreams into reality? I've got three key tips:

1. Work Hard: As my father advised me years ago, if you want anything, work hard for it. I've lived by this principle throughout my life. Whether it's acquiring houses, cars, or anything else, I have achieved it through my hard work. However, it's not just about working hard; it's also about doing the right things.
2. Surround Yourself with the Right People: None of us can achieve our dreams alone. Building a reliable team, both at the strategic and operational levels, is crucial. Surround yourself with people who can support and work with you to bring your dreams to fruition.
3. Secure the Right Funding: To secure the right funding, you need to have accurate financial information. Understand your current situation, historical data, and most importantly, where you're

headed with forecasts. Engage with funders, demonstrating that you have the right team, a solid strategy, and you will find funding.

Reflect on your dreams: What are your most cherished dreams or aspirations? Write them down and explore why they are important to you.

Consider your work ethic: How hard are you currently working to achieve your dreams? Are there areas where you could improve or optimise your efforts?

Evaluate your support system: Who are the people around you? Assess your personal and professional networks. Are they supportive and aligned with your goals? Identify areas where you might need to strengthen your team.

Financial awareness: How well do you understand your current financial situation? What steps can you take to enhance your financial knowledge and ensure you have the right information to attract funding for your dreams?

Relaxation and self-care: In what ways do you prioritise relaxation and self-care? Consider incorporating activities that rejuvenate you into your routine for a more balanced approach to achieving your dreams.

Happiness

I love talking about happiness. Do you?

It's been another good week, with some challenging things going on as ever, but there's been more funding secured and another Know Your Numbers group started. There has been lots of great feedback and things this week, and all that makes me happy. When I see the interaction amongst the group that started on Thursday, it's just amazing to hear the things that they've picked up already, having just been on a session for a couple of hours. So that makes me happy.

Various other good client things are happening as well, and it's just been a week of happiness. I've made some other changes in my personal life. If anyone's been following my posts, there are some other things happening there that are making me happy too. And I'm going to my granddaughter's dancing display tomorrow. This will be her first dancing display. She's three, and that will remind me of the days when I used to take both of my daughters. So that's happening tomorrow, and that makes me happy as well.

I try to spend every day being happy, and I hope you can too.

Reflect on the moments in your life that bring you happiness. How can you incorporate more of these into your daily or weekly routine?

Consider recent accomplishments or positive experiences that contributed to your happiness. How did these achievements make you feel, and how can you build on them for future happiness?

Explore the changes you've made in your personal or professional life that contribute to your happiness. Are there other areas where you can make positive changes to enhance your overall well-being?

Listening

I believe that listening is an area where we could all improve. There are times when I realise, I should be more attentive to what's happening. Interestingly, the letters in the word "listen" are the same as in the word "silent." Staying silent makes it easier for us to listen.

I've often told my kids that if they truly listen, they might learn something. When you're talking, you're merely sharing what you already know or think you know. However, if you take the time to be silent and listen, you might gain valuable insights. It's a skill I've been actively working on for many months, and I believe we can all enhance our listening abilities. I'll keep it short and sweet so that you don't have too much to listen to. Have a great weekend, and make sure to actively listen to your loved ones.

Reflect on a recent situation where you felt you could have listened better. What were the consequences, and how might active listening have improved the outcome?

Consider a time when someone listened to you attentively. How did it make you feel, and what impact did it have on your communication with that person?

Identify specific strategies or techniques you can employ to enhance your listening skills. How can you create a more receptive and attentive environment in your personal and professional interactions?

Fulfilment

Do you feel fulfilled with what you're doing on a day-to-day basis? I certainly do. This week has been fantastic, filled with many positive developments. It's been a bit hectic, but I've successfully navigated through it. We had another great Know Your Numbers clinic with a new group that started last month. Witnessing people learn and already apply new insights to their businesses, looking at numbers differently, and posing excellent questions about margins, EBITDA, and funding is truly rewarding. It gives me a warm and fuzzy feeling.

Additionally, I welcomed a couple of new clients this week, and it's wonderful to see positive changes in their approaches, even though we've only just begun. There are also exciting things happening with existing clients, and the feedback has been overwhelmingly positive. The overall trajectory is fantastic, and I feel fulfilled about the progress.

On a personal note, I received a lovely email from Gregoire, a student I sponsor in Congo pursuing an engineering degree. His heartfelt message, along with one from his father, brought a tear to my eye. Being able to contribute in this way brings me a deep sense of fulfilment.

Reflect on a recent accomplishment or positive development in your life or work. How did it make you feel, and what aspects of it contributed to your sense of fulfilment?

Consider an activity or project you're currently involved in. Assess your level of fulfilment in relation to it. Are there aspects you can adjust or enhance to increase your overall sense of satisfaction?

Explore ways in which you can incorporate more fulfilling experiences into your routine. Whether personal or professional, identify actions you can take to bring a greater sense of purpose and satisfaction to your daily life.

You Get What You Tolerate

"You get what you tolerate." If you think about it, if you put up with something, things are unlikely to change. So, if you've put up with a customer's poor payment patterns, if you put up with an employee doing the same thing, and you've got to cover for their mistakes, or something in your personal life where someone is treating you poorly, if you continue to put up with that and you tolerate it, that's what you'll continue to get. Because there is unlikely to be any change from the other side.

But if you stand up to it and you do something about it, then it might change. If you speak to a customer and you say, "No, our terms are 30 days, we're not accepting payment in 47." If you say to your employee, "No, you keep not doing that thing properly, I keep having to do something about it. Here's what you do." If you have a relationship with someone and they keep doing something you don't like or you're not happy with, if you don't tell them, they're unlikely to change as well.

That is why if you just keep doing what you're doing, you tolerate it, then you'll continue to get the same thing. And it's like Einstein said, that if you keep doing the same thing over and over and expecting different results, that's the sign of madness. And I must confess I do have certain elements in my life that I've changed recently because I was doing the same thing or other people were doing the same thing, and things weren't changing. If you tolerate it, it will continue.

My advice to you is, if it's things that you do want to change, you need to do something about it. So don't tolerate it. Stand up, do something about it.

Reflect on areas in your life where you have tolerated certain behaviours or situations. How have these tolerances influenced your experiences, and what changes would you like to make?

Consider a recent instance where you stood up and acted against something you were tolerating. How did it feel, and what positive outcomes resulted from your decision?

Explore your approach to communication when dealing with issues you tolerate. Do you find it challenging to express your dissatisfaction or set boundaries? How can you improve your assertiveness in such situations?

PART 12: UNDERSTANDING

Gaining insight and understanding of your business landscape is vital. This chapter delves into the importance of knowledge, market insight, and informed decision-making.

NOTES

Measuring, Monitoring, and Managing

How important is measuring, monitoring, and managing in business?

I personally go for a bi-annual health check. My doctor does blood checks, weight, height, and various other things. I learned recently that my metabolic age has increased by five years. I am 52 and my metabolic age is 41. Six months ago, my metabolic age was only 36. Only through measuring, managing, and monitoring did I realise that I have not looked after myself as well as I should over the last six months. With that knowledge, I can work on my health more diligently.

Consider your business. What can happen in six months if you are not regularly measuring and monitoring your results? How can you manage if you don't measure and monitor? How can you manage if you don't Know Your Numbers? How can you make decisions based on incomplete information? What you are doing is you are operating in a vacuum. At best, you are either guessing or trying to use your instincts.

When it comes to managing your business, you owe it to yourself to make sure that you have the information you need to make sound business decisions.

In our Know Your Numbers sessions, we focus on understanding where you are, where you have been, and where you are going. We focus on making sure our members have the right profit and loss, balance sheet, cash flow, and the right forecasts.

On a personal note, I have made some changes. Basically, I am doing things that I should have done a few months ago.

My doctor pointed out to me that inflammation is a major problem in my body. I can ignore it and hope for the best, or I can measure and manage it for better health. The choice seems obvious to me.

What do you need to measure, monitor, and manage better in your business to help you Know Your Numbers?

What is your next step to improving your ability to measure, monitor, and manage your business?

Which area of your business is the most critical for you to start measuring and monitoring?

Feelings

Our lives are driven by feelings. One of the things I discuss regularly with people is how does your business make you feel. For many, they're worried, stressed, and unsure. A lot of that happens because they don't have the right people around them, they don't have the right information. That can cause all sorts of problems with their personal life as well.

You end up spending time at the weekend with your kids at swimming, dancing, or football, and you might be present, but you're not actually there. When you go out for dinner with your partner on Saturday evening, again, you're not there because you're thinking about the week ahead, thinking about the things that you need to deal with that you're worried about.

This week, we're releasing five testimonial videos from Know Your Numbers. One of the great things about them is the change it's made in terms of how people feel because they now have control, funding, and the ability to understand things and put things in place. I got emotional talking about feelings when I was watching the initial drafts of the video. I was in the car when I was in Crete, and it made me cry because of the impact it had on the people involved in that video.

I really want to stress that you can get rid of worry, stress, and all these negative feelings in your business by doing the right thing, surrounding yourself with the right people, speaking to the right people, and Knowing Your Numbers. There's a lot of information out there, and if you don't make the change, then you will be permanently stuck in that place.

I got a photograph from a client this morning. He sent me a photograph of the bank statement. Less than three years ago, he was turning over half a million pounds. We exceeded two million pounds the first year I got involved. I'm a shareholder in the business. The photo he sent me this morning shows that we have more cash than we had turnover just about two and a half years ago, with almost seven figures in the bank.

Now I know how that makes him feel. I know how that makes me feel. I want to encourage people to make the change, do these things, and you will feel so much better in your business, your personal life, your relationships.

Reflect on the impact of your business on your personal life and relationships. How does it make you feel, and are there changes you can make to improve that?

Consider the role of control and funding in your business. What steps can you take to enhance your control and financial stability?

Reflect on a moment in your business journey that made you emotional. How did that moment influence your perspective and decisions?

Responsibility

When I mention responsibility, I'm specifically referring to the responsibility regarding your numbers, financial position, cash flow, and everything else related. I've received a couple of comments and engaged in discussions this week, particularly after the launch of the new Know Your Numbers group. The Know Your Numbers Mastery program is set to launch in November, and if you haven't heard or applied yet, well, why not?

Now, about responsibility, I've encountered a couple of business owners stating, "Well, I don't need to because I've got a bookkeeper, or I've got an accountant, or I've hired someone else to look after that." To use a technical term, it's not specifically finance, but that's complete and utter nonsense. At the end of the day, you bear the responsibility for your business—it's your business, it's your wealth, and it's tied up in that business.

What's the cost of making a decision wrong because you haven't understood the financial position, or you haven't specifically known your numbers in a certain area? Think about that. Consider getting your margins wrong by 10% or pricing wrong by not setting the right level or making incorrect decisions because you lacked proper visibility. What was the cost of that?

Moreover, when you plan to exit, how can you possibly engage in proper discussions with someone looking to buy your business if you can't sit and have a comprehensive financial discussion with them, using high-level numbers? So, take responsibility for your numbers. If you're a business owner, it's not difficult. I know accountants and finance directors like to make it seem mysterious, but, again, don't buy into that notion; it's also nonsense. It's straightforward.

This is precisely why I developed Know Your Numbers—to educate business owners. For too long, business owners have been kept in the dark. It's easy for you to take responsibility. You don't need to know everything, but you need to understand key financial statements, forecasts, and funding—all covered in Know Your Numbers. The ability to apply that knowledge in your business and make better decisions is fantastic. I know it makes a difference. It will improve your profitability, cash flow, and shareholder value.

How do you currently handle the financial responsibility of your business, considering your understanding of numbers, financial position, and cash flow?

Think about a past decision in your business where a lack of financial understanding might have influenced the outcome. What was the cost of not having proper visibility, and how could a better grasp of your numbers have changed that decision?

Consider your approach to financial responsibility. Are there aspects of financial statements, forecasts, or funding that you feel less confident about? What steps can you take to improve your understanding and make more informed decisions for your business?

Growing

As we all know, if you are not growing, you are dying. If you think of nature, when plants stop growing, they start dying. This principle applies to us as individuals. If we are not growing and improving, then ultimately, we are on a decline.

All my clients are growing; they are ambitious, which is why I am working with them. If I think of the latest Know Your Numbers Mastery group which started this week, there is a new group with 12 people, all ambitious and working in growing businesses. They want to develop themselves in terms of knowing their numbers because they understand the difference it can make for their business going forward. Knowing your numbers is crucial for getting the right funding in place.

There was a client I was working with that I mentioned a few weeks ago, where I managed to secure them a half-million-pound confidential invoice financing facility. However, they subsequently chose not to take it, and decided not to pay me. Today, I found out that they have not paid someone else working for them, to the tune of about £10,000. They now have a CCJ against them, which will hinder their growth and impede them from getting the necessary funding and supplier credit.

It's quite sad and entirely unnecessary. I encourage people to continue growing, build a team around you that will support your growth, ensure you Know Your Numbers, and get the right funding in your business. This will enable you to continue growing.

Reflect on a time in your life when you experienced significant personal or professional growth. What factors contributed to that growth, and how did it shape your trajectory?

Consider the importance of Knowing Your Numbers in your current endeavours, whether personal or professional. How does having a clear understanding of your financial metrics impact your decision-making and overall success?

Explore the concept of building a supportive team around you. Have you experienced the positive effects of collaboration and teamwork in your pursuits? How has a supportive team contributed to your growth and success?

It Is Never Too Late

It is never too late. That's based on a couple of meetings I have had this week with business owners who are in their 50s. They have decided either that they want to better understand the numbers, or they want to grow the business.

They have engaged with me through the latest Know Your Numbers group and separately to work with me to help them grow their business and to educate them. They have picked that up by watching some videos, listening to other people, and observing other businesses that have been at a similar level to them but have gone on and grown over the last couple of years.

They are sitting, wondering, "Wait a minute, what are we missing here?" So, they have engaged either as a group or working with me one-to-one because they are ambitious, and they want to move their business to the next level. It doesn't matter whether you are in your 20s, 30s, 40s, 50s, or whatever age it may be. It is never too late to Know

Your Numbers and to think about growing your business and getting the right funding and information in place.

Reflect on a time when you decided to pursue a new goal or venture later in life. What motivated you to take that step, and how did it impact your personal or professional development?

Consider the importance of continuous learning and adaptation in your life. How have you stayed open to new ideas, like the business owners mentioned in the text, who engaged to better understand their numbers and grow their businesses?

Explore the concept of ambition and its role in personal and professional growth. How has ambition driven your decisions and actions in the past, and how do you envision it influencing your future endeavours?

Same Place Next Year

Do you want to be in the same place next year? What I mean by that is, are you thinking about growing this year? Do you want to be in the same place you started the year, or do you want to be somewhere different from a business perspective, and from a personal perspective? If the answer to that is yes, what are you doing about it?

One of the things you should be thinking about is improving everything in general, surrounding yourself with the right people, looking at individuals you see as role models, people you admire, people you aspire to be, and getting the right people within your team. It's important to do that because the companies I see growing the most are doing just that. They are getting the right people, doing the right things, learning new things.

We have a new Know Your Numbers group starting soon, and I can see from the previous two groups the differences it makes to the information, decisions, and, as a result, profitability, and cash flows. It's hugely important.

Alongside getting the right people in your team, aim for those you aspire to be.

Reflect on your aspirations for the year. Do you envision being in the same place next year, or are you striving for growth and change? What specific actions can you take to move toward your desired outcomes?

Consider the importance of surrounding yourself with the right people, as mentioned in the text. Who are the role models and individuals you admire in your field or life? How can you incorporate their influence and guidance into your journey?

Explore the impact of continuous learning and improvement on your personal and professional growth. Are there specific areas where you can invest in learning and skill development this year? How might this contribute to your overall success and fulfilment?

Get It Done

Do you get it done? How many of you decided on the 31st of December or the first of January to do something and have you kept doing it, or have you stopped already in terms of getting things done?

Are you keeping yourself accountable, or is someone else keeping you accountable? One of the things I'm known for in business is that if I say I'll get something done, I get it done. It doesn't matter if I need to work all day, work all night, or work the weekend, whatever that may be. My reputation is about getting things done for my clients, and it applies in your personal life as well.

If you say you're going to do things, do you keep yourself accountable? Is someone else keeping you accountable? I'm pretty good at getting things done.

The one thing I failed in last year is learning Greek, and that's basically because I've not had the brainpower and the brain capacity to do it. So, what I've done today is I have signed up for a Greek group class because that will make me more accountable. Hopefully, they will accept me, and this time next year, I'll be speaking a lot more Greek.

Think about yourself, think about your business. The things that you've said you'll do but haven't. Get it done. That's an ongoing theme for me.

Reflect on a specific goal or task you set for yourself at the beginning of the year. Have you been consistent in working towards it, or have you encountered challenges? What steps can you take to recommit and get it done?

Consider the importance of accountability in achieving your goals, as mentioned in the text. How do you hold yourself accountable, and are there ways you can enhance this accountability? Alternatively, are there individuals or groups that can support and hold you accountable?

Explore any areas in your personal or professional life where you may have fallen short in the past year. What strategies can you implement to overcome obstacles and ensure that you get things done in those areas moving forward?

Focus on Yourself

Do you focus on yourself? I'm fed-up hearing people comparing themselves to other people or complaining about what other people are doing. You see on LinkedIn regularly, people complaining about the 5 am Club or the 4 am Club. If somebody wants to be up at 4 am in the gym or in a barrel of cold water and are doing whatever they want to do, it has absolutely nothing to do with you. If that works for them, let them go on with it.

Why don't you just focus on yourself? You might work at the other end of the day. So, focus on that. Too many people compare themselves to other people, not with a view to improving or emulating them and doing what they're doing to make themselves successful, but to be critical or to complain.

And I see it all the time. So, it's a bit of a rant today because if you can focus on yourself and just get on with the things you need to go on with, you'll be in a much better position than you will be just sitting there competing and complaining about other people.

Just aim for your own targets, for your own goals. It doesn't matter what the person next door or the company next door is doing or anybody else, do what's right for you. And just let the other people get on with what's right for them. Live and let live.

Reflect on a time when you found yourself comparing your lifestyle or habits to someone else's. What emotions did it evoke, and how did it impact your mindset?

Consider an area of your life where you tend to criticise or complain about others rather than seeking inspiration or learning from their success. How might shifting your focus toward self-improvement benefit you?

Explore your personal goals and targets. Are they driven by your authentic desires, or are they influenced by external expectations or comparisons with others? How can you enhance your focus on self-improvement and personal growth?

Success

Success means different things to different people; it could be houses, cars, money in the bank, status, titles, and all those sorts of things. For me, it's quite simple. Success is about happiness and freedom to make my own choices.

Simple as that. Yes, it's nice to have money, houses, cars, holidays, and all these things, but without the happiness and the ability to make your own choices, your own decisions, then I don't think that's success. I'm going to keep it short and sweet this week because I am running late for various things.

Define success in your own terms. What does it mean to you, and what elements contribute to your sense of accomplishment and fulfilment?

Reflect on a time when you achieved a goal or milestone. How did it impact your overall happiness, and did it provide a sense of freedom or autonomy in your choices?

Consider the balance between external markers of success (e.g., material possessions, status) and internal factors (e.g., happiness, freedom) in your life. Are there adjustments you'd like to make to align your definition of success more closely with your values and priorities?

Control

There are certain things that we can control; we can't control the weather, but we can control our attitude towards it. We can't control what other people think about us or what they do, but we can control our responses to that. In our business as well, we can control finance. We can be on top of finance, on top of cash by having the right information and managing it properly. We can be in control of our team and people by managing them properly and building the right team around us.

For me, it's about attitude. I think life and business are about your attitude. There are certain things you can control, and there are certain things you can't, but if you can focus on the things you can control, you will go far.

Reflect on a recent situation where you couldn't control external factors. How did you manage your attitude and response to it?

Consider your approach to financial management in your business. What steps can you take to improve your control over finances?

Think about your team management skills. How can you enhance your ability to lead and build a strong team around you?

NOTES

PART 13: RESOURCEFULNESS

Innovation and creative problem-solving are at the heart of entrepreneurship. Explore how to be resourceful, think outside the box, and leverage available resources for your business.

NOTES

Loneliness

I want to talk about loneliness, triggered by the fact that Maria has been away for just over a week now. It does make things quite lonely. It's a bit like running your own business when you're the person in charge, making all the decisions; that can be very lonely as well. I speak to many CEOs and business owners who have no one to talk to, no one to run things past. That's often why I end up getting involved with their business as well.

If it was easy, everybody would be doing it, and nobody would have employment. Running your own business is not easy; it comes with many challenges. There are always many things to deal with. It's great if you can surround yourself with the right people, with a team, non-executives, an advisor, or just someone you can talk to so that it's not lonely. What happens is people often bottle things up, and then it all comes out at the wrong time. You can avoid that by not being lonely, by having people around that can help you through it.

Reflect on a time when you felt lonely in your professional or personal life. How did it impact your well-being and decision-making? What strategies did you use to cope with loneliness?

Consider the analogy of running a business and the potential loneliness that comes with it. Do you currently have a support system or people to discuss business challenges with? How might building a network of support positively influence your business journey?

Explore the concept of bottling up emotions and the impact it can have. Have there been instances where you kept concerns to yourself, only for them to surface later? How can you cultivate an environment where open communication is encouraged to prevent such situations?

Opportunity

I have spoken about opportunity before. I keep hearing people complaining that they do not have enough opportunities, or they cannot get labour, or they lack cash. Well, the flip side of that is I am working with many companies who have an abundance of opportunities. The reason for that is they are going out and doing things. They are taking action, doing the hard work, putting in place systems and procedures.

I have one client who has booked orders of more than they turned over in the full year last year. They've done that in the space of about three and a bit months. They've also enhanced their gross margin significantly because of a change in the way they do things. I've got another client who is sitting on a potential opportunity that will more than double his business, already a seven-figure business.

These people are going out and making things happen. I really want to encourage people to go out and do that. I keep talking about Knowing Your Numbers; it is important. For me, it is the foundation of your business. If you Know Your Numbers, you will be able to manage things better. If you manage things better, you can monitor them better, make changes, and with funding in place, you can take advantage of opportunities.

This morning, I had an invoice finance audit with a client. We are looking to double the facility because we have an abundance of opportunities. We sailed through that audit; it took us 30 minutes. In some cases, these audits will take a whole day. The reason for that is we were well-prepared, had the right information, and now this company can just rock on and take advantage of these opportunities.

Reflect on the opportunities you currently have in your business. Are there untapped possibilities waiting to be explored?

How well do you know the financial numbers of your business? Reflect on how this knowledge can be a foundation for better management.

Consider a recent challenge or opportunity in your business. How could having proper funding and financial preparation impact your ability to navigate and seize such situations?

I Am Back and I Am Giving Back

I am back and I am giving back. Previously, I talked about being back from Athens, and I discussed being back both mentally and physically, emphasising my return to the gym.

As I read the British Business Bank Intermediaries report, highlighting how companies often lack proper financing, and many business owners are unaware of it, it made me reflect. There's a significant quote in the report that resonated with me, stating, "I think there's a lot of bad advice out there."

This sentiment aligns with my perspective, where I often criticise accountants, FDs, and advisors in general for not providing the necessary advice and being productive enough. While I acknowledge that I'm not perfect, I focus on what works for my clients.

Moving forward, I've decided to offer three free sessions every month to growing and ambitious business owners who aren't receiving the advice they need. I aim to guide them in the right direction, whether it's related to funding or obtaining essential information from their accountants.

I've witnessed the positive impact of joining Know Your Numbers on people's businesses and personal lives, and I want to extend this assistance to those who may not be able to access it.

Reflect on a time when you felt the need for better advice or guidance in your business or personal life. How did you navigate the situation, and what difference would it have made if you had access to the right advice?

Consider the quote, "I think there's a lot of bad advice out there." How do you discern between good and bad advice in your life? Are there specific sources or criteria you rely on when seeking guidance?

Imagine receiving three free sessions to address your business challenges or personal development. What areas of your life or business would you prioritise, and how might this support positively impact your growth and ambitions?

Commitment

Tony Robbins talks about passion being the genesis of genius. He states that what happens with most people is that they run out of fuel, and the fuel is basically hunger and commitment.

When I think about the clients I work with, I've met with several of them this week. They exhibit an extraordinary level of hunger and commitment. Most of these individuals have started their ventures, perhaps due to redundancy, and have built up their teams. They have shown immense commitment, drive, and determination, whether they've started from scratch or transitioned from something different.

My client base is filled with people like that, and I love working with individuals who embody such qualities because that's the spirit I resonate with. I've done everything myself, not having the privilege of a fortunate upbringing. I recognise that all my achievements stem from hard work, success, and determination.

Even examining my own business over the last couple of years, last year saw a 50% increase in turnover. In the first four months of this year, I've grown by 66%, a bit of a surprise to me, but it aligns with the number of hours and efforts I've been putting in.

To anyone watching this and contemplating their own position, remember that you ultimately determine your success, as Tony says, through commitment, passion, and hunger. Combine all these elements, and success will follow. In the end, you don't achieve much by sitting and doing nothing.

I conclude nearly all my LinkedIn posts with "take action and drive success." Because, at the end of the day, if you don't act, success won't follow. While luck may play a part, I'm a firm believer in taking control of the process yourself, be it in business or your personal life, dealing with challenges, or navigating through life's uncertainties.

Just get on with it, make the commitment, show the hunger and passion, and you'll get there.

Reflect on a time in your life when you demonstrated exceptional commitment and determination. What were the outcomes of your efforts, and how did that experience shape your perspective on success?

Consider the role of passion and hunger in your current pursuits, whether personal or professional. How can you further cultivate these qualities to enhance your commitment and drive toward success?

In moments of challenge or uncertainty, how do you typically respond? Reflect on your approach to acting and driving success. Are there areas where you could amplify your commitment and passion to achieve better outcomes?

All or Nothing

All or nothing. What does that mean to you? Anyone who knows me knows I am pretty much an all or nothing person. I'm not in-between. It's something that I seem to have done all throughout my life. I can think of learning various things and immersing myself in it.

One reason I gave up alcohol four years ago today is because I was very much all in on that. There was always an excuse to have a drink; I wasn't dependent on it, but I really enjoyed it, and I was very good at it. And I practised a lot at it!

The same goes for many other things. I'm learning Greek now, practising it every day for a couple of hours, having two lessons a week with a tutor. It's pretty much all in for me. It would be great to do more, but I need to sacrifice some more sleep, and I don't really sleep enough as it is.

I do the same with my exercise. When I'm working out, I'm not thinking about people in their 50s; I'm thinking about being the best I can be and competing against, in my own mind, people who are a lot younger than me. That's just the standards I set for myself. It's the same in business with my clients. I'm all in; I'm either with them or not. It doesn't matter if I get a phone call at 10 o'clock on a Tuesday morning or three o'clock on a Saturday afternoon. If they need me to do something, it happens. And those who work with me know that.

That's why I pride myself on discernment. I played poker and learned how to play poker 10-15 years ago. I bought about 50 books, immersed myself in it. Before I knew it, I was playing in professional tournaments, qualifying for about $5 when others were paying $500-$1000 to get in. It was funny because I ended up knowing more than many of the professional players I was playing with.

So, all or nothing is just the mindset. It's the same with business. In my own business, I always keep saying I won't take on more things and end up doing it because I love doing what I'm doing. I am all in, in my business. And when I see the people I'm working with, they are very much all in as well, whether they're working all the hours or not taking money out or guaranteeing things (which I really don't like, but sometimes it has to happen). That's the kind of people I like spending my time with and working with.

The theme for me: all or nothing. If you're going to do something, do it well. I remember my father telling me many years ago, "If you want to do something, do it properly." That was while colouring in a drawing for a Boys' Brigade thing. I hadn't really coloured it in well, and he told me, "Look, do it properly, make sure it's all filled in properly, make it all nice and blue." It stuck with me forever. So, if you're going to do something, do it, do it well, commit to it, and be all in.

Reflect on a specific instance in your life where you embraced an "all or nothing" approach. What was the outcome of your commitment, and how did it shape your experience?

Consider areas in your life where you might adopt more of an "all or nothing" mindset. How could this approach positively impact your pursuit of goals or personal growth?

Explore the concept of discernment and how it plays a role in your decision-making. Reflect on situations where discernment has been crucial and consider how it aligns with an "all or nothing" philosophy.

Reflecting

I've been reflecting on that as I sit here, pondering what the coming weeks are going to bring. I reflect a lot. I like to look at where I've come from, where I've been, and where I'm going. I visited my first home last Saturday. I was visiting my mother, and on the way to where she lives now, which was my second home, I stopped at the council flats where I was brought up.

Now they've been demolished; there were four large towers, and they've been demolished. It just lets me understand where I came from, where I am now. I then drove to my mother's home, my second home. I moved from the council flat to this house, and thought, "Wow, this is amazing." And it was at the time. But then, as I reflect looking back, it's about what you're used to.

I do the whole reflection thing myself as well, just in terms of what I've done over the last few years to where I am and what's happening now. As I say, I have no idea what else I'm talking about today because my brain has been pretty much fried. Reflecting on this week has been an amazing week; there have been so many great things happening. I've got so many things happening with clients. We're raising money, increasing facilities, buying businesses, bringing in new teams of people— all sorts happening, and it's just fantastic.

I've had a couple of nights without a huge amount of sleep, but that's fine. And I will keep doing that. As people have been saying to me for many years, "How long can you keep running at this pace." Well, look what I'm still doing. So, reflect yourself, on where you are, where you've been and where you're going.

Reflect on a specific moment in your life when revisiting a place from your past triggered a deep reflection. What insights did you gain about your journey and personal growth?

Consider a recent week or time where you felt overwhelmed with activities and events. How did you navigate through it, and what positive aspects emerged from the chaos?

Explore your own approach to reflection. How frequently do you take time to look back on your experiences, and how does it contribute to your personal and professional development?

Lead a Horse to Water

You can lead a horse to water, but you can't make it drink. This seems appropriate given the recent rain in Glasgow. As I write this, it's currently raining, and I'll be heading to horse racing later in the afternoon, or at least I will be by the time this gets posted.

What I mean by "you can lead a horse to water" is about providing advice and opportunities for change. You can guide people, suggesting things they can and should do, but you can't force them to act. You can take them to the water, but you can't make them drink. While you can offer advice, the decision to make changes ultimately rests with the business owner and the individuals involved in the business. If they choose not to act, nothing changes, and the business remains in the same place.

I've witnessed the impact of businesses not heeding the right advice, refusing available funding, and later regretting those decisions. This regret may stem from the business becoming insolvent, missing out on opportunities due to a lack of funding, or investing time in projects with low margins. Taking the right advice and seizing opportunities is crucial.

So, if you find yourself at the water's edge, make sure to take a drink.

Reflect on a time when you were given valuable advice or an opportunity for change. Did you embrace it, or did you hesitate? What were the outcomes of your decision?

Consider a situation where you provided advice or opportunities for change to someone else, whether in your personal or professional life. How did they respond, and what impact did it have on their situation?

Explore any instances where you resisted taking advice or making a necessary change. What factors influenced your decision, and what were the consequences? How can you approach such situations differently in the future?

Staying Calm

I have a reputation for being calm. Very rarely will you see me stressed. I would be surprised if any of you out there have seen me stressed. My clients do not see me stressed. They do not see me angry; they do not see me annoyed. It is just the way I live my life. And I find it is much easier that way.

One of the ways to do that is if you can control something, then do something about it. If you can do something about it, do not worry, and do not stress. So, you stay calm. Now, if you cannot do something about it, well, you cannot do something about it. So do not stress, do not worry, and stay calm. It is quite a simple way of living your life. It works for me. Do not get me wrong, I am not one hundred percent perfect on it. But generally, that is how my life goes.

And today, I am feeling absolutely fantastic, completely not stressed, perfectly calm, and just had a great few weeks. Feeling good. And I am chilling today, doing various personal things, which is great.

So, my advice to you over the course of the weekend is to stay calm.

Reflect on a recent situation where you remained calm in the face of stress. How did you manage to maintain your composure, and what impact did it have on the outcome of the situation?

Think about an area in your life where you struggle to stay calm. What triggers your stress in this area, and what strategies could you employ to approach it more calmly?

Describe a day in your ideal life where you feel 'absolutely fantastic, completely not stressed, and perfectly calm.' What activities are you doing, and what makes this day so fulfilling for you?

Short Cuts

I am sure you have all seen shortcuts: get-rich-quick schemes, 30 days for six-pack abs, learn Greek in a week, all this nonsense. It just does not happen. It does not work.

I have always been a great believer in putting the hard work in, by doing the right things, not necessarily just working hard. If you work hard at the wrong things, you will not get anywhere. But if you work hard and do the right things, then you do not need these get-rich-quick schemes, or Fast Tracks, because, in general, it just does not work. You have got to learn, you have got to understand, you have got to do things.

It is the same when you are running your business. You have got to do the right things. There is no quick and easy fix for success. You have got to make sure you are doing all the right things, you have all the right people, and you have the right funding, all of these things.

For many people, you have probably heard that before they achieved "overnight" success it took many years. And that is very true, because very few people just turn around and become an overnight success. There are many, many, many hard hours, lots of graft, lots of challenges, taking on risks, going without things.

So, do not look for the quick fix. I am assuming that most of you who watch this are not the quick-fix type of person. If you are, take my advice: it does not work. Get to the hard work and do the right things. Have the right plan, surround yourself with great people. Make sure you have the right funding, the right support, and you will go so much further forward.

Reflect on a time when you were tempted by a shortcut or an easy solution. What did you learn from this experience about the value of hard work and perseverance?

Think about a project or goal where you chose to put in the hard work instead of looking for a quick fix. How did this decision impact the outcome and your personal growth?

Consider the statement, "You have got to learn, you have got to understand, you have got to do things." How does this apply to your current challenges or goals, and what are the key actions you need to take to achieve success?

NOTES

PART 14: MEET CRAIG ALEXANDER RATTRAY

With a career spanning three decades, Craig Alexander Rattray isn't your average Finance Director/Chief Financial Officer. He's a strategic thinker, a master with financial strategies that work, an expert at raising finance, and driving rapid business growth.

His unrivalled blend of skills – developed in private equity/venture capital investment management – along with his background as a Scottish Chartered Accountant means that Craig Alexander brings a wealth of insight and skill to the growth-focused companies he works with.

Craig Alexander thrives on supporting companies experiencing change and challenge, including early-stage development, growth, new market entry, acquisitions, and scale-ups as well as positioning for exit.

His focus is unwavering: to drive profitability, improve cash flow, and massively increase shareholder value.

He launched Know Your Numbers: a programme designed to help business owners dramatically improve their financial and business acumen, and improve the profits and cash flow in their business (https://knowyournumbers.biz/)

He is the author of Mastering Cash Flow: How Business Owners Can Banish Stress & Sleepless Nights, And Secure Funding For Growth available on Amazon, and free PDF at https://masteringcashflowbook.com.

PART 15: WHAT OUR ENTREPRENEURS SAY

NOTES

Craig Alexander loves working with entrepreneurs and that comes across in how THEY think and talk about him. Here are just a few of the things they've shared after working with him.

"Instant impact on my company"

"Craig, as a human being, has been incredibly supportive, he's open, picking up the phone to make sure I'm okay and helping me with my problems - which just wasn't what I expected. It's just how good Craig is as a human being!"

"Craig probably doesn't understand the debt that I owe him – just by him being him – and also giving me the training to help me get through my recent events."

"Craig was to the point, he made things very simple. When I discussed my issues with my business, he was immediately looking at ways to help and, for me, he added a significant amount of value before I even joined… and I thought well if I can speak to him for half an hour and get that value from him, then over a six month period I'm pretty sure I'll get a lot more!"

"You need someone like Craig in your corner."

"Works at a different level to anyone I have previously engaged with financially."

"He is truly inspirational and exudes energy."

"Had me feeling worthy, motivated and ready to take on the world."

"Everything's more focused now. Focused on clients, on profitable business. We're now very good at deciding what work we want and what kind of work, more importantly, we don't want!"

"It's like putting your glasses on and everything stops being fuzzy and comes into focus!"

"His energy exudes and rubs off on the others."

"It has been one of the highlights of our year, Craig, having you involved. Not just business, personally too. You are a force of nature and an inspiration. We are so privileged to have you in our lives. Onwards and upwards together!"

"Every business owner knows what a lonely place it can be, making all the decisions, wondering if you're doing the right thing, lacking expertise in different areas. Joining Craig Alexander on the programme has been an eye opener. I can't stress enough how valuable it is to have a group of your peers helping with you work through your business challenges. Thanks Craig Alexander!"

"I have been working with Craig Alexander for only two months and the changes to me and my business are amazing. He is truly inspirational and exudes energy. I have already freed up time and can see the building blocks of value taking shape. I am excited to continue the journey with him."

PART 16: THE KNOW YOUR NUMBERS FRAMEWORK

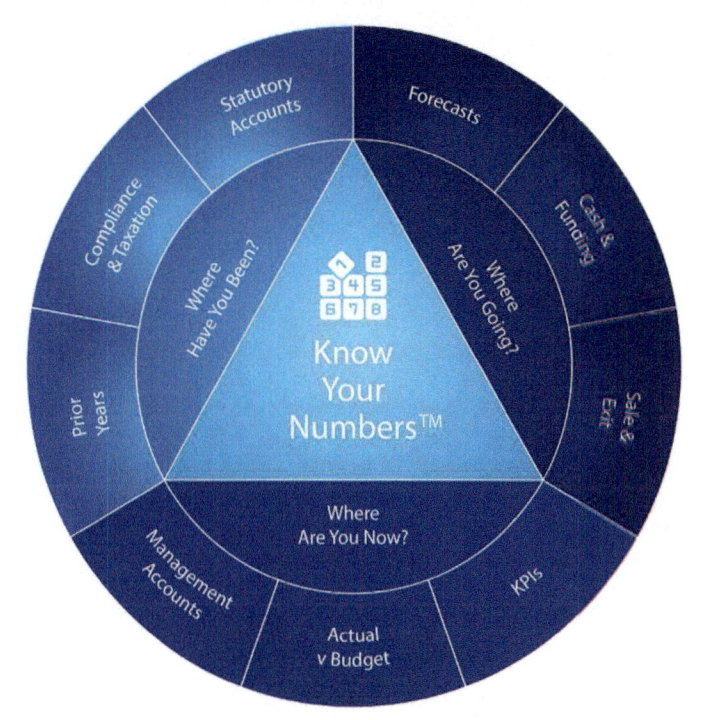

The Know Your Numbers (KYN) Framework helps you understand:

- Where have you been?
- Where are you going?
- Where are you know?

Knowing Your Numbers means that you will always have the confidence you need to make sound business decisions.

Learn more about Know Your Numbers at: https://knowyournumbers.biz.

What was your biggest takeaway as you read this book?

_____

_____

_____

_____

_____

_____

What are your immediate action steps for your business?

_____

_____

_____

_____

_____

_____

_____

_____

_____

_____

_____

PART 17: FINAL THOUGHTS FROM THE ROCKING CHAIR

As we conclude our journey through "Rocking Chair Wisdom," we reflect on the diverse and dynamic nature of entrepreneurship. From the strategic intricacies of economic planning to the personal resilience required to navigate business challenges, each theme has offered unique insights and valuable lessons. Whether it's about building networks, managing finances, or upholding ethical standards, the journey of an entrepreneur is rich with learning and growth. Remember, entrepreneurship is not just a business venture; it's a personal voyage of discovery, growth, and fulfilment. Keep these themes close to your heart as you continue your path, and may they guide you to success and satisfaction in your entrepreneurial endeavours.

To your success!

Craig Alexander Rattray

https://craigalexanderrattray.com

Email: ca@craigalexanderrattray.com

LinkedIn: https://www.linkedin.com/in/craig-alexander-rattray

NOTES

NOTES

WANT MORE WISDOM?

When you're ready, here are three other ways I can help you help yourself:

ONE: Learn from my KYN Learning Academy

Learn from our short video series why 'Knowing Your Numbers' will help you stop financial firefighting, cut your stress, and help grow your business.

knowyournumbers.biz/kyn-training-academy

TWO: Take the online Cash Flow Diagnostic Scorecard:

Are you ready to uncover the hidden risks in your cash flow? Answer 10 questions to find out.

kyncashflowdiagnostic.com

THREE: Take your learning to the next level and join a Know Your Numbers Mastery Group

Join Craig and a small group of other entrepreneurs on a journey to get less stress, more profit and to make better decisions.

knowyournumbers.biz/know-your-numbers-mastery-group

See you on the other side, Craig!

Lessons From the Rocking Chair

Printed in Great Britain
by Amazon